Ninja Flip

Air Fryer

Cookbook with Color Pictures

Flavorful & Hassle-Free Ninja Flip Air Fryer Recipes to Upgrade Your Cooking Game | Endless Recipe Possibilities in One Flip

Poppy Power

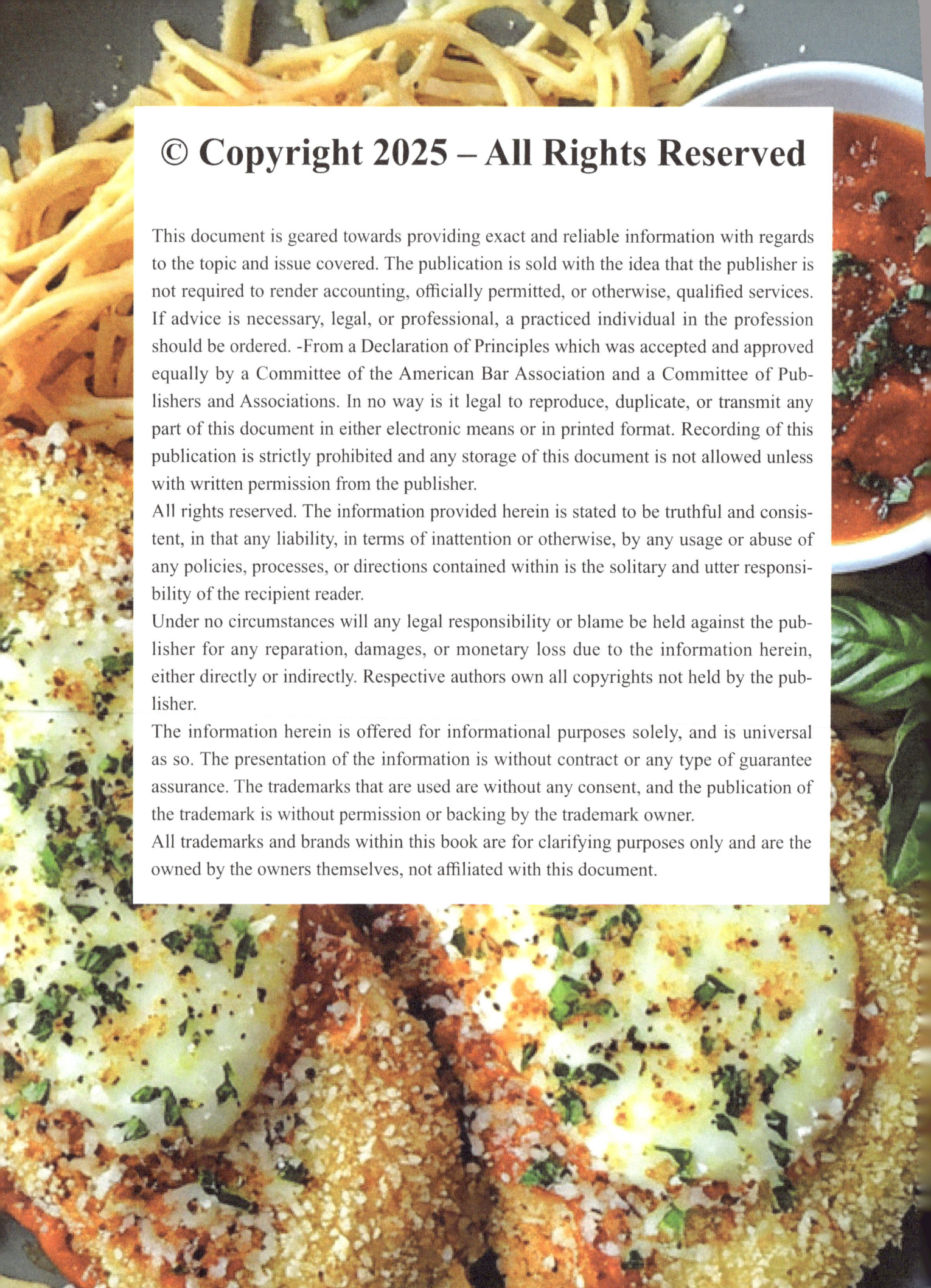

© Copyright 2025 – All Rights Reserved

This document is geared towards providing exact and reliable information with regards to the topic and issue covered. The publication is sold with the idea that the publisher is not required to render accounting, officially permitted, or otherwise, qualified services. If advice is necessary, legal, or professional, a practiced individual in the profession should be ordered. -From a Declaration of Principles which was accepted and approved equally by a Committee of the American Bar Association and a Committee of Publishers and Associations. In no way is it legal to reproduce, duplicate, or transmit any part of this document in either electronic means or in printed format. Recording of this publication is strictly prohibited and any storage of this document is not allowed unless with written permission from the publisher.

All rights reserved. The information provided herein is stated to be truthful and consistent, in that any liability, in terms of inattention or otherwise, by any usage or abuse of any policies, processes, or directions contained within is the solitary and utter responsibility of the recipient reader.

Under no circumstances will any legal responsibility or blame be held against the publisher for any reparation, damages, or monetary loss due to the information herein, either directly or indirectly. Respective authors own all copyrights not held by the publisher.

The information herein is offered for informational purposes solely, and is universal as so. The presentation of the information is without contract or any type of guarantee assurance. The trademarks that are used are without any consent, and the publication of the trademark is without permission or backing by the trademark owner.

All trademarks and brands within this book are for clarifying purposes only and are the owned by the owners themselves, not affiliated with this document.

Table of Contents

1	Introduction 1
2	Fundamentals of Ninja Flip Toaster Oven & Air Fryer 2
3	4-Week Meal Plan 7
4	Chapter 1 Breakfast Recipes 9

- 9 Lemony Blueberry Muffins
- 9 Avocado and Egg Breakfast Bagel
- 10 Crispy Breakfast Quesadilla
- 10 Cheesy Olive and Roasted Pepper Bread
- 11 Jalapeño Popper Egg Cups
- 11 Egg-Loaded Potato Skins
- 12 Breakfast Calzone
- 12 Cranberry Orange Muffins
- 13 Ham and Egg Cups
- 13 Ham and Cheese Pastries
- 14 Cheesy Bell Pepper Eggs
- 14 Sausage Cheddar Scones
- 15 French Toast Casserole
- 15 Sausage Cheese Balls
- 16 Cinnamon Rolls with Cream Cheese Glaze
- 16 Cherry Tomato Avocado Toast

5	Chapter 2 Vegetable and Side Recipes 17

- 17 Zucchini Salad with Feta and Parsley
- 17 Mini Hasselback Potatoes
- 18 Lemon Thyme Asparagus
- 18 Cauliflower Steak with Gremolata
- 19 Ratatouille Vegetables
- 19 Healthy Bell Pepper Salad
- 20 Shishito Peppers with Sour Cream Dipping Sauce
- 20 Herbed Shiitake Mushrooms
- 21 Roasted Rosemary Potatoes
- 21 Carrots with Cumin-Orange Vinaigrette
- 22 Veggie Burgers
- 22 Sweet and Sour Brussels Sprouts
- 23 Sesame Green Beans
- 23 Spicy Vegetable and Tofu
- 24 Parsnip Fries with Romesco Sauce
- 24 Cheesy Broccoli Sticks

6	Chapter 3 Snack and Appetizer Recipes 25

- 25 Dry Rub Chicken Wings
- 25 Crispy Parmesan Artichokes
- 26 Bacon-Wrapped Jalapeño Poppers
- 26 Mozzarella Sticks
- 27 Crispy Nacho Avocado Fries
- 27 Smoked Salmon & Cream Cheese Bagel
- 28 Popcorn Chicken Bites
- 28 Classic Pepperoni Pizza
- 29 Sausage Stuffed Mushrooms
- 29 Cauliflower Buffalo Bites with Blue Cheese Dipping Sauce
- 30 Bacon-Wrapped Tater Tots
- 30 Sweet and Spicy Nuts
- 31 Crispy Ranch Pickles
- 31 Loaded Zucchini Skins
- 32 Crab and Cream Cheese Wontons
- 32 Crispy French Fries

7	Chapter 4 Poultry Recipes 33

- 33 Paprika Chicken Wings
- 33 Easy Chicken Fajitas

34	Classic Chicken Parmesan
34	Crispy Chicken Nuggets
35	Cilantro Lime Chicken Thighs
35	Honey-Glazed Turkey Tenderloins with Carrots and Snap Peas
36	Buffalo Turkey Meatballs
36	Bacon-Wrapped Stuffed Chicken Breasts
37	Parmesan Chicken Fingers
37	Spiced Chicken Drumsticks
38	Chicken Cordon Bleu
38	Crispy Chicken Cutlets
39	Honey Mustard Turkey Burgers
39	Crispy Chicken Meatballs
40	Lebanese Turkey Burgers with Tzatziki
40	Tandoori Chicken Breasts
41	Buffalo Chicken Tenders
41	Pickle Brined Fried Chicken

8 Chapter 5 Beef, Pork, and Lamb Recipes … 42

42	Barbecued Riblets
42	Flavorful Pork Milanese
43	Italian Stuffed Bell Peppers
43	Greek Meatballs with Tzatziki Sauce
44	Poblano Pepper Cheeseburgers
44	Mediterranean-Style Lamb Meatballs
45	Shawarma Lamb Loin Chops and Potatoes
45	Chinese-Style Pork Spareribs
46	Pesto Pork Chops
46	Roasted Beef and Vegetables
47	Herbed Lamb Burgers
47	Blue Cheese Sirloin Steak Salad
48	Thai Beef Satay with Peanut Sauce
48	Flank Steak with Tomato Corn Salsa
49	Chicken-Fried Steak with Gravy
49	Parmesan Pork Chops

9 Chapter 6 Fish and Seafood Recipes … 50

50	Crispy Coconut Shrimp
50	Halibut Tacos
51	Maple-Balsamic Glazed Salmon
51	Broiled Tuna Steaks with Roasted Asparagus
52	Roasted Cod with Mixed Vegetables
52	Garlic Lemon Scallops
53	Crispy Parmesan Tilapia
53	Chilean Sea Bass with Olive Relish
54	Homemade Catfish Strips
54	Fish Fillets with Lemon-Dill Sauce
55	Crispy Fish and Chips
55	Crispy Tuna Patties
56	Crab Cakes
56	Savory Tandoori Shrimp
57	Smoked Salmon Phyllo Triangles
57	Simple Buttered Cod Fillets

10 Chapter 7 Desserts Recipes …………… 58

58	Mini Apple Hand Pies
58	Brownie Bites
59	Soft Pretzels
59	Cream Cheese Cookies
60	Carrot Cake with Cream Cheese Icing
60	Buttermilk Biscuits
61	Nutella & Strawberry Toast
61	Lemon Blueberry Scones
62	Mini Chocolate Nut Pies
62	Hasselback Apple Crisp
63	Air Fried Beignets
63	Peanut Butter Banana Toast
64	Ham and Cheese Croissants
64	Authentic Struffoli
65	Nutmeg Butter Cookies
65	Crispy Coconut Bananas with Pineapple Sauce

11 Conclusion ………………………………… 66

12 Appendix 1 Measurement Conversion Chart   67

13 Appendix 2 Recipes Index   …………… 68

Introduction

Are you ready to transform the way you cook? Imagine having one versatile appliance that can air fry, air roast, broil, bake, bagel, toast, pizza, and more—all with minimal effort and maximum flavor. Welcome to the Ninja Flip Air Fryer Cookbook with Color Pictures, your ultimate guide to unlocking the full potential of your Ninja Flip Toaster Oven & Air Fryer. Whether you're a busy parent, a health-conscious foodie, or someone who just loves quick, delicious meals, this cookbook is designed with you in mind.

Inside, you'll find a collection of vibrant, easy-to-follow recipes with stunning color photos that make every dish irresistible. From crispy breakfasts and hearty lunches to mouthwatering dinners and guilt-free snacks, we've covered it all. Each recipe is crafted to help you achieve perfect textures and bold flavors using the Ninja Flip Toaster Oven & Air Fryer's unique cooking functions.

No more guesswork! We provide clear step-by-step instructions, precise cooking times, and expert tips to ensure consistent, delicious results. Plus, the ingredients are simple and accessible, making meal prep stress-free. Ready to flip your cooking game? Let's dive into a world of quick, crispy, and flavorful dishes that will wow your family and friends!

Fundamentals of Ninja Flip Toaster Oven & Air Fryer

The Ninja Flip Toaster Oven & Air Fryer is a versatile kitchen appliance designed to meet the demands of modern cooking. Its innovative flip design allows it to function as both a traditional toaster oven and a powerful air fryer, saving space while maximizing efficiency. With multiple cooking functions—including bake, broil, toast, bagel, air fry, air roast, and dehydrate—you can prepare a wide range of meals with ease.

Equipped with advanced heating technology, it ensures even cooking and crisp results every time. The adjustable temperature and timer controls provide precision, while the flip-up feature makes storage simple, freeing up valuable counter space. Whether you're making crispy fries, golden toast, or perfectly baked goods, the Ninja Flip Toaster Oven & Air Fryer delivers fast, healthy, and delicious results with minimal effort.

What is Ninja Flip Toaster Oven & Air Fryer?

The Ninja Flip Toaster Oven & Air Fryer is a cutting-edge, multifunctional kitchen appliance designed to simplify and elevate your cooking experience. Unlike traditional toaster ovens, it combines the capabilities of an air fryer with the versatility of a compact oven, allowing you to cook a variety of dishes with one device. Its unique flip-up design not only saves counter space but also adds a sleek, modern touch to your kitchen.

Equipped with eight-in-one functions, this multifunctional device can air fry, air roast, bake, broil, toast, bagel, dehydrate, and pizza—you can effortlessly prepare everything from crispy snacks and perfectly toasted bagels to juicy roasts and golden-brown desserts. The powerful convection fan ensures rapid, even cooking, reducing the need for excess oil and promoting healthier meals.

The Ninja Flip Toaster Oven & Air Fryer is equipped with intuitive controls, including precise temperature and time settings, making it easy to adjust for any recipe. Its large interior capacity fits air fryer basket, wire rack, and sheet pan, while the crumb tray and nonstick surfaces simplify cleanup.

Ideal for busy individuals, health-conscious cooks, and families alike, this appliance is perfect for quick breakfasts, weekday dinners, and weekend treats. Whether you're air frying chicken wings, baking cookies, or toasting your morning bread, the Ninja Flip Toaster Oven & Air Fryer delivers consistently delicious results, transforming everyday cooking into a fast, flavorful, and stress-free experience.

Getting to Know the Control Panel

The Ninja Flip Toaster Oven & Air Fryer is a versatile appliance equipped with multiple functions to simplify your cooking needs. Each function is designed to deliver consistent and delicious results with minimal effort. Let's understand its control panel.

Cooking Functions:

Air fry: Perfect for making fast, extra-crispy foods like chicken wings, French fries, and chicken nuggets. Requires little to no added oil, making it a healthier option for fried foods without sacrificing flavor or crunch.

Air roast: Ideal for achieving a crispy exterior and juicy interior on foods like sheet pan meals, thicker cuts of meat, and roasted vegetables. Ensures even cooking throughout, perfect for hearty family dinners.

Bake: Designed for even baking of cookies, brownies, cakes, and more. Great for achieving golden-brown crusts and soft, fluffy textures.

Pizza: Cooks frozen or homemade pizzas evenly for a crispy crust and melty toppings. Ideal for quick pizza nights at home.

Broil: Perfect for broiling meats and fish, giving a beautiful sear or caramelized finish. Also great for evenly browning the tops of casseroles or gratins.

Toast: Can evenly toast up to 6 slices of bread at once. Customize the level of browning (shade) to suit your taste preferences.

Bagel: Designed to perfectly toast up to 6 bagel halves. Focuses heat on the cut-side while gently warming the outside for the perfect bagel texture.

Dehydrate: Gently removes moisture from foods, ideal for making healthy snacks like dried fruits, jerky, and vegetable chips.

Operating Controls:

Power Button: Press to turn the unit on or off. Holds the central control function to start or end your cooking sessions.

MODE +/- Button: Selects your desired cooking function (Air Fry, Air Roast, Bake, etc.). Press + or – to toggle through the available functions.

TEMP/SHADE +/- Buttons: Adjusts the cooking temperature for most functions. When using Toast or Bagel mode, these buttons adjust the shade level (browning intensity) instead of temperature.

TIME/SLICES +/- Buttons: Adjusts the cooking time for precise results. In Toast or Bagel mode, these buttons change the number of slices instead of time. The display shows countdowns in minutes and seconds for times under 1 hour, and in hours and minutes for times over 1 hour.

START/STOP Button: Press to start or stop the cooking process at any time. Allows you to pause and resume as needed.

Light Button: Turns the interior oven light on or off. The light automatically turns on during the last 30 seconds of cooking for easy monitoring.

Time & Temperature Display: Shows the current cooking time and temperature.

Displays helpful indicators:

PRE: Oven is preheating.

SHADE/SLICES: Active in Toast or Bagel functions to adjust browning or slice quantity.

Flip Icon: Indicates when the oven is cool enough to flip up for cleaning or storage.

HOT: Alerts when the oven is still hot to the touch even after cooking is complete.

STOP: Displays if the oven is flipped during cooking (not recommended). Refer to the user manual's Error Messages & FAQ section for more guidance.

By understanding these functions and controls, you'll be able to maximize the versatility of your Ninja Flip Toaster Oven & Air Fryer for perfect results every time—whether you're air frying crispy snacks, baking desserts, or preparing quick breakfasts!

Benefits of Using Ninja Flip Toaster Oven & Air Fryer

Multifunctional Design for Versatile Cooking

The Ninja Flip Toaster Oven & Air Fryer isn't just one appliance—it's many. With settings for baking, air frying, broiling, toasting, dehydrating, air roasting, and more, it handles everything from crispy fries to tender roasts. This all-in-one capability means you can replace multiple kitchen gadgets, saving both space and money.

Space-Saving Flip-Up Design

Its unique flip-up design allows you to store it vertically when not in use, freeing up valuable counter space. Perfect for small kitchens, apartments, or anyone looking to declutter, this feature ensures your kitchen remains organized without sacrificing functionality.

Faster Cooking Times

Thanks to its powerful convection fan and rapid heating elements, the Ninja Flip Toaster Oven & Air Fryer cooks food up to 60% faster than traditional ovens. This efficiency means you can prepare quick meals during busy weekdays without compromising on quality or taste.

Healthier Cooking with Less Oil

Air frying technology uses hot air circulation to achieve crispy, golden textures without the need for deep frying in oil. This results in meals with less fat and fewer calories, making it an excellent choice for health-conscious individuals who still crave delicious, crunchy foods.

Even, Consistent Results Every Time

The advanced heating system ensures even temperature distribution, preventing hot spots and ensuring consistent cooking results. Whether you're baking cookies or roasting vegetables, you'll enjoy perfectly cooked food every time.

Energy Efficient

The compact size and rapid preheat time make it more energy-efficient than full-sized ovens. You'll save on electricity while still being able to bake, roast, and air fry your favorite meals. Plus, it generates less heat, keeping your kitchen cooler—perfect for warm weather.

User-Friendly Controls

The intuitive control panel features easy-to-use dials and buttons for adjusting time, temperature, and cooking functions. Whether you're a beginner or an experienced cook, you'll find it simple to operate, making meal prep quick and hassle-free.

Easy Cleanup

Designed with nonstick surfaces, removable crumb trays, and dishwasher-safe accessories, the Ninja Flip Toaster Oven & Air Fryer makes cleanup a breeze. Spend less time scrubbing and more time enjoying your meals with family and friends.

Large Capacity in a Compact Design

Despite its small footprint, the interior is spacious enough to fit a 13-inch pizza, six slices of toast, or a variety of baking pans. This makes it suitable for both small households and larger gatherings, offering flexibility without taking up too much space.

Perfect for Every Meal

From breakfast to dinner—and even dessert—the Ninja Flip Toaster Oven & Air Fryer has you covered. Toast bagels to perfection, whip up crispy chicken wings, bake fluffy muffins, or dehydrate fruits for healthy snacks. Its versatility makes it a must-have for any kitchen, encouraging creativity and inspiring delicious new recipes.

Before First Use

To ensure your Ninja Flip Toaster Oven & Air Fryer is ready for safe and optimal performance, follow these detailed steps for initial setup and preparation.

Unpack the Appliance:

1. Carefully open the packaging box and remove the Ninja Flip Toaster Oven & Air Fryer from its protective materials.
2. Discard any packaging materials such as plastic wraps, foam inserts, cardboard spacers, promotional labels, and securing tape that may be attached to the unit. These materials are used for protection during shipping and should not be kept.

Remove Accessories and Review the Manual:

1. Take out all included accessories from the package. This may include the air fry basket, sheet pan, wire rack, and removable crumb tray.
2. Read the user manual thoroughly. Pay special attention to the operational instructions, safety warnings, and important safeguards. Understanding these guidelines helps you operate the appliance correctly, reducing the risk of injury, accidents, or damage to the unit.

Clean the Accessories:

1. Before using the appliance for the first time, it's important to clean all detachable parts to remove any residue from manufacturing or packaging.
2. Wash the air fry basket, sheet pan, wire rack, and removable crumb tray using warm, soapy water. Use a soft, non-abrasive sponge to gently scrub the surfaces and avoid scratching them.
3. Rinse thoroughly with clean water to remove any soap residue.
4. Dry all parts completely with a soft towel or allow them to air dry before reassembling.

Important: Do NOT place the sheet pan in the dishwasher, as it may damage the non-stick coating or warp the metal. Handwashing is recommended for the sheet pan.

Clean the Main Unit:

1. Use a damp cloth or sponge to gently wipe down the exterior and interior walls of the main unit to remove any dust or residue from the manufacturing process.
2. NEVER submerge the main unit in water or any other liquid. This appliance contains electrical components that can be severely damaged if exposed to moisture.
3. Do NOT place the main unit in the dishwasher under any circumstances.

By following these steps, you'll ensure that your Ninja Flip Toaster Oven & Air Fryer is clean, safe, and ready for optimal performance.

How to Use Ninja Flip Toaster Oven & Air Fryer?

Air Fry

1. Press the MODE +/- buttons until AIR FRY lights up. The default time and temperature will appear.
2. Use the TIME/SLICES +/- buttons to set the cooking time, up to 1 hour, adjusting in 1-minute increments.
3. Press the TEMP/SHADE +/- buttons to choose a temperature between 250°F and 450°F, adjusting in 5-degree increments.
4. Press the START/STOP button to start preheating.
5. Place ingredients in the air fry basket. For fatty, oily, or marinated foods, position the basket on the top rails and slide the sheet pan with the wire rack on the bottom rails. For dry foods, use just the air fry basket. Shake or rotate the basket halfway through cooking for even results.
6. When the unit beeps to signal preheating is done, slide the basket onto the upper rails. If using the sheet pan, place it on the bottom rails.
7. For even browning and crispiness, shake or rotate the basket halfway through the cooking cycle.
8. When the cooking time is complete, the unit will beep, and "END" will appear on the display.

Air Roast

1. Press the MODE +/- buttons until AIR ROAST lights up. The default time and temperature will appear on the display.
2. Use the TIME/SLICES +/- buttons to set the cooking time, up to 2 hours. Time adjusts in 1-minute increments for under 1 hour and 5-minute increments for over 1 hour.
3. Adjust the temperature between 250°F and 450°F using the TEMP/SHADE +/- buttons, with 5-degree increments.
4. Press the START/STOP button to start preheating. Place your ingredients on the sheet pan.
5. When the unit beeps to indicate it's preheated, open the oven door and place the sheet pan on the wire rack in the bottom rails. Close the oven door.
6. During cooking, you can open the oven door to check or flip the ingredients as needed.
7. When the cooking time ends, the unit will beep, and "END" will display.

Bake

1. Press the MODE +/- buttons until BAKE lights up. The default time and temperature will appear on the display.
2. Use the TIME/SLICES +/- buttons to set the cooking time, up to 2 hours. Time adjusts in 1-minute increments for under 1 hour and 5-minute increments for over 1 hour.
3. Adjust the temperature between 250°F and 450°F using the TEMP/SHADE +/- buttons, with 5-degree increments.
4. Press the START/STOP button to start preheating.
5. Place your ingredients on the sheet pan. When the unit beeps to indicate it's preheated, place the sheet pan on the wire rack in the bottom rails and close the oven door.
6. During cooking, you can open the oven door to check or flip the ingredients as needed.
7. When the cooking time ends, the unit will beep, and "END" will display.

Pizza

1. Press the MODE +/- buttons until PIZZA lights up. The default time and temperature will appear on the display.
2. Use the TIME/SLICES +/- buttons to set the cooking time, up to 2 hours. Time adjusts in 1-minute increments for under 1 hour and 5-minute increments for over 1 hour.
3. Adjust the temperature between 180°F and 450°F using the TEMP/SHADE +/- buttons, with 5-degree increments.
4. Press the START/STOP button to start preheating.

5. Place your pizza on the sheet pan or wire rack. When the unit beeps to indicate it's preheated, place the sheet pan on the wire rack in the bottom rails and close the oven door.
6. During cooking, you can open the oven door to check on the pizza.
7. When the cooking time ends, the unit will beep, and "END" will display.

Broil
1. Press the MODE +/- buttons until BROIL lights up. The default time and temperature settings will appear.
2. Use the TIME/SLICES +/- buttons to set the cooking time, up to 30 minutes, adjusting in 10-second increments.
3. Adjust the temperature using the TEMP/SHADE +/- buttons to select either HI (450°F) or LO (400°F).
4. Place your ingredients on the sheet pan, then position the pan on the wire rack in the bottom rails. Close the oven door and press the START/STOP button to start cooking.
5. During cooking, you can open the oven door to check or flip the ingredients as needed.
6. When the cooking time ends, the unit will beep, and "END" will appear on the display.

Toast
1. Press the MODE +/- buttons until TOAST lights up. The default settings for the number of slices and shade level will be displayed.
2. Use the TIME/SLICES +/- buttons to select the number of bread slices, up to 6 slices at once.
3. Adjust the browning level using the TEMP/SHADE +/- buttons to choose your preferred shade.
4. Place the bread slices on the wire rack positioned in the bottom rails. Close the oven door and press the START/STOP button to start toasting.
5. When toasting is complete, the unit will beep, and "END" will appear on the display.

Bagel
1. Press the MODE +/- buttons until BAGEL lights up. The default settings for the number of slices and shade level will be displayed.
2. Use the TIME/SLICES +/- buttons to select the number of bagel halves, up to 6 halves at once.
3. Adjust the browning level using the TEMP/SHADE +/- buttons to choose your preferred shade.
4. Place the bagel halves, cut-side up, on the wire rack positioned in the bottom rails. Close the oven door and press the START/STOP button to start toasting.
5. When toasting is complete, the unit will beep, and "END" will appear on the display.

Dehydrate
1. Press the MODE +/- buttons until DEHYDRATE lights up. The default time and temperature settings will appear on the display.
2. Use the TIME/SLICES +/- buttons to set the desired time, up to 12 hours, adjusting in 15-minute increments.
3. Adjust the temperature using the TEMP/SHADE +/- buttons, selecting between 85°F and 200°F, with 5-degree increments.
4. Place the ingredients in the air fry basket and slide the basket into the top rails of the oven. Close the oven door and press the START/STOP button to start dehydrating.
5. During the process, you can open the oven door to check or flip the ingredients for even drying, especially halfway through the cycle.
6. When the dehydrating time is complete, the unit will beep, and "END" will display, signaling that your food is ready.

With these easy-to-follow instructions, your Ninja Flip Toaster Oven & Air Fryer will become an essential part of your daily kitchen routine, delivering perfect results every time!

Cleaning and Caring for Ninja Flip Toaster Oven & Air Fryer

Proper cleaning and maintenance of your Ninja Flip Toaster Oven & Air Fryer are essential for ensuring its optimal performance and longevity. Follow these detailed steps to clean the appliance thoroughly after each use.

Everyday Cleaning
1. **Unplug the Unit:** Make sure the appliance is unplugged and completely cooled before you start cleaning.
2. **Clean the Crumb Tray:** Slide out the crumb tray when the oven is flipped down. Empty it after every use. Hand wash if needed.

3. **Wash Accessories:** Clean the air fry basket, wire rack, and other accessories after each use. Hand washing is recommended to prevent wear, especially for the air fry basket and wire rack. Do NOT put the sheet pan in the dishwasher.
4. **Wipe Interior:** Use a soft, damp sponge to clean any food splatters inside the oven. Avoid abrasive cleaners, scrubbing brushes, or harsh chemicals as they can damage the oven.
5. **Clean Exterior:** Wipe down the outer surface and control panel with a damp cloth. For stubborn stains, use a mild, non-abrasive liquid cleaner applied to the cloth (never directly on the oven).
6. **Important Notes:** Empty the crumb tray frequently. DO NOT submerge the unit in water or place it in the dishwasher.

Flip-Up-and-Away Storage

1. **Cool Before Flipping:** Only flip the unit up when it's cool. The display will show FLIP when it's safe. Wait until the fan stops running (about 15 minutes after cooking) before unplugging.
2. **Flip Carefully:** Use the side handles to lift and flip the unit upward.

Deep Cleaning

1. **Unplug and Cool:** Always let the unit cool and unplug it before cleaning.
2. **Remove and Wash Accessories:** Take out all accessories, including the crumb tray. Hand wash or soak in hot, soapy water overnight. Use a non-abrasive brush for thorough cleaning. The air fry basket and wire rack can go in the dishwasher, but may wear faster over time.
3. **Clean Interior:** Wipe the inside with warm, soapy water and a soft cloth. Never use abrasive materials or harsh chemicals.
4. **Hand Wash for Longevity:** To extend the life of accessories, always hand wash when possible.
5. **Dry Completely:** Make sure all parts are thoroughly dry before putting them back in the oven.
6. **Important Note:** Never immerse the main unit in water or place it in the dishwasher.
7. **Storage Tip:** Store the unit in the upright position with accessories inside to save space and for easy deep cleaning.

Tips for Using Ninja Flip Toaster Oven & Air Fryer

Maximize your Ninja Flip Toaster Oven & Air Fryer's performance and achieve the best results with these helpful tips. Whether you're air frying, toasting, baking, or broiling, these guidelines will ensure consistent, delicious outcomes every time.

Use the Right Accessories:

Air Fry Basket: Ideal for foods that need crisping, like fries, chicken wings, or vegetables.
Sheet Pan: Best for baking cookies, roasting meats, or catching drips when air frying greasy foods.
Wire Rack: Perfect for toasting bread, bagels, or baking pizzas.
Maximize Airflow for Crispier Results: Arrange food in a single layer with space between pieces to allow hot air to circulate. Overcrowding can lead to uneven cooking.
Shake or Flip Midway: For even browning, shake the basket or flip ingredients halfway through cooking, especially when air frying or roasting.
Monitor Toast & Bagels Closely: Use the SHADE setting to adjust crispness. Start with a lower setting for lighter toasting and adjust based on preference.
Keep It Clean: Empty the crumb tray regularly to prevent burning odors. Wipe down the interior with a damp cloth after each use to avoid buildup.
Adjust Cooking Times: The Ninja Flip Toaster Oven & Air Fryer cooks faster than traditional ovens. Check food a few minutes before the suggested time to prevent overcooking.

Cool Before Flipping for Storage: Wait until the unit displays FLIP and cools down completely before flipping it for storage. This helps maintain the appliance's longevity.
Experiment with Dehydrate Mode: Try dehydrating fruits, vegetables, or even making homemade jerky. Cut foods evenly and keep them spaced out for the best results.
Don't Forget the Light Button: Use the oven light to check food progress without opening the door, helping maintain consistent temperatures during cooking.
Use a Thermometer for Accuracy: When cooking meats, use a meat thermometer to ensure proper internal temperatures for food safety.
Utilize Leftover Heat: After cooking, the residual heat is perfect for warming plates or keeping food warm without extra energy use.
Try Reheating Leftovers: Skip the microwave—reheat pizza, fries, or chicken in the air fryer for crisp, fresh-like results. Use a lower temperature for gentle reheating.

By following these tips, you can enjoy consistent, high-quality results with your Ninja Flip Toaster Oven & Air Fryer every time.

Frequently Asked Questions

Q: Do I need to preheat the oven before cooking?
A: Yes, for optimal results, especially when baking, roasting, or air frying. The unit will beep when preheating is complete. Some functions, like broiling and toasting, don't require preheating.

Q: Can I use the sheet pan instead of the air fry basket with the Air Fry function?
A: Yes, but flipping ingredients during cooking is required, and levels of crispiness may vary.

Q: Can I cook frozen foods directly without thawing?
A: Yes, the Ninja Flip Toaster Oven & Air Fryer is great for cooking frozen foods. You may need to adjust the cooking time slightly for even results.

Q: Is it safe to flip the oven up while it's cooking?
A: No, it's strongly recommended NOT to flip the oven during cooking. Wait until the unit cools down, and "FLIP" appears on the display.

Q: Can I put the sheet pan or air fry basket in the dishwasher?
A: The air fry basket and wire rack are dishwasher safe but may wear faster over time. The sheet pan should be hand-washed.

Q: Why does "STOP" appear on the display during cooking?
A: This happens if the oven is flipped up during cooking, which is not recommended. If it appears without flipping, contact Customer Service.

Q: Can I toast bagels and bread at the same time?
A: Yes, but for best results, place bagels cut-side up and adjust the shade setting accordingly for even toasting.

Q: Why is steam or water dripping from the door?
A: This is normal, especially when cooking high-moisture foods. Steam vents from the door, and condensation may drip onto the counter.

Q: How do I reset the oven to its default settings?
A: Press and hold the START/STOP and LIGHT buttons together for 5 seconds to restore factory settings.

Q: Why does the fan keep running after I turn off the oven?
A: The cooling fan continues to run until the unit's temperature drops below 95°F. This is normal and helps protect the oven's internal components.

4-Week Meal Plan

Week 1

Day 1:
Breakfast: Lemony Blueberry Muffins
Lunch: Mini Hasselback Potatoes
Snack: Crispy Nacho Avocado Fries
Dinner: Classic Chicken Parmesan
Dessert: Mini Apple Hand Pies

Day 2:
Breakfast: Avocado and Egg Breakfast Bagel
Lunch: Zucchini Salad with Feta and Parsley
Snack: Bacon-Wrapped Jalapeño Poppers
Dinner: Roasted Beef and Vegetables
Dessert: Brownie Bites

Day 3:
Breakfast: Cheesy Bell Pepper Eggs
Lunch: Spicy Vegetable and Tofu
Snack: Dry Rub Chicken Wings
Dinner: Broiled Tuna Steaks with Roasted Asparagus
Dessert: Soft Pretzels

Day 4:
Breakfast: Sausage Cheddar Scones
Lunch: Sweet and Sour Brussels Sprouts
Snack: Mozzarella Sticks
Dinner: Cilantro Lime Chicken Thighs
Dessert: Cream Cheese Cookies

Day 5:
Breakfast: Crispy Breakfast Quesadilla
Lunch: Lemon Thyme Asparagus
Snack: Crispy Parmesan Artichokes
Dinner: Poblano Pepper Cheeseburgers
Dessert: Carrot Cake with Cream Cheese Icing

Day 6:
Breakfast: Cherry Tomato Avocado Toast
Lunch: Cauliflower Steak with Gremolata
Snack: Popcorn Chicken Bites
Dinner: Roasted Cod with Mixed Vegetables
Dessert: Buttermilk Biscuits

Day 7:
Breakfast: Cinnamon Rolls with Cream Cheese Glaze
Lunch: Sesame Green Beans
Snack: Smoked Salmon & Cream Cheese Bagel
Dinner: Shawarma Lamb Loin Chops and Potatoes
Dessert: Nutella & Strawberry Toast

Week 2

Day 1:
Breakfast: Breakfast Calzone
Lunch: Veggie Burgers
Snack: Classic Pepperoni Pizza
Dinner: Honey-Glazed Turkey Tenderloins with Carrots and Snap Peas
Dessert: Lemon Blueberry Scones

Day 2:
Breakfast: Jalapeño Popper Egg Cups
Lunch: Ratatouille Vegetables
Snack: Sausage Stuffed Mushrooms
Dinner: Italian Stuffed Bell Peppers
Dessert: Mini Chocolate Nut Pies

Day 3:
Breakfast: Egg-Loaded Potato Skins
Lunch: Cheesy Broccoli Sticks
Snack: Bacon-Wrapped Tater Tots
Dinner: Maple-Balsamic Glazed Salmon
Dessert: Hasselback Apple Crisp

Day 4:
Breakfast: Cheesy Olive and Roasted Pepper Bread
Lunch: Shishito Peppers with Sour Cream Dipping Sauce
Snack: Cauliflower Buffalo Bites with Blue Cheese Dipping Sauce
Dinner: Pickle Brined Fried Chicken
Dessert: Air Fried Beignets

Day 5:
Breakfast: Cranberry Orange Muffins
Lunch: Herbed Shiitake Mushrooms
Snack: Sweet and Spicy Nuts
Dinner: Halibut Tacos
Dessert: Authentic Struffoli

Day 6:
Breakfast: French Toast Casserole
Lunch: Parsnip Fries with Romesco Sauce
Snack: Sweet and Spicy Nuts
Dinner: Greek Meatballs with Tzatziki Sauce
Dessert: Ham and Cheese Croissants

Day 7:
Breakfast: Ham and Cheese Pastries
Lunch: Healthy Bell Pepper Salad
Snack: Loaded Zucchini Skins
Dinner: Herbed Lamb Burgers
Dessert: Peanut Butter Banana Toast

Week 3

Day 1:
Breakfast: Ham and Egg Cups
Lunch: Roasted Rosemary Potatoes
Snack: Crab and Cream Cheese Wontons
Dinner: Bacon-Wrapped Stuffed Chicken Breasts
Dessert: Nutmeg Butter Cookies

Day 2:
Breakfast: Sausage Cheese Balls
Lunch: Carrots with Cumin-Orange Vinaigrette
Snack: Crispy French Fries
Dinner: Chinese-Style Pork Spareribs
Dessert: Crispy Coconut Bananas with Pineapple Sauce

Day 3:
Breakfast: Lemony Blueberry Muffins
Lunch: Zucchini Salad with Feta and Parsley
Snack: Bacon-Wrapped Jalapeño Poppers
Dinner: Crispy Coconut Shrimp
Dessert: Mini Apple Hand Pies

Day 4:
Breakfast: Avocado and Egg Breakfast Bagel
Lunch: Mini Hasselback Potatoes
Snack: Dry Rub Chicken Wings
Dinner: Lebanese Turkey Burgers with Tzatziki
Dessert: Brownie Bites

Day 5:
Breakfast: Cheesy Bell Pepper Eggs
Lunch: Spicy Vegetable and Tofu
Snack: Crispy Nacho Avocado Fries
Dinner: Thai Beef Satay with Peanut Sauce
Dessert: Soft Pretzels

Day 6:
Breakfast: Sausage Cheddar Scones
Lunch: Sweet and Sour Brussels Sprouts
Snack: Mozzarella Sticks
Dinner: Garlic Lemon Scallops
Dessert: Cream Cheese Cookies

Day 7:
Breakfast: Crispy Breakfast Quesadilla
Lunch: Lemon Thyme Asparagus
Snack: Crispy Parmesan Artichokes
Dinner: Mediterranean-Style Lamb Meatballs
Dessert: Carrot Cake with Cream Cheese Icing

Week 4

Day 1:
Breakfast: Cherry Tomato Avocado Toast
Lunch: Cauliflower Steak with Gremolata
Snack: Popcorn Chicken Bites
Dinner: Chicken Cordon Bleu
Dessert: Buttermilk Biscuits

Day 2:
Breakfast: Cinnamon Rolls with Cream Cheese Glaze
Lunch: Sesame Green Beans
Snack: Smoked Salmon & Cream Cheese Bagel
Dinner: Flank Steak with Tomato Corn Salsa
Dessert: Nutella & Strawberry Toast

Day 3:
Breakfast: Breakfast Calzone
Lunch: Veggie Burgers
Snack: Classic Pepperoni Pizza
Dinner: Crispy Fish and Chips
Dessert: Lemon Blueberry Scones

Day 4:
Breakfast: Jalapeño Popper Egg Cups
Lunch: Ratatouille Vegetables
Snack: Sausage Stuffed Mushrooms
Dinner: Honey Mustard Turkey Burgers
Dessert: Mini Chocolate Nut Pies

Day 5:
Breakfast: Egg-Loaded Potato Skins
Lunch: Cheesy Broccoli Sticks
Snack: Bacon-Wrapped Tater Tots
Dinner: Chicken-Fried Steak with Gravy
Dessert: Hasselback Apple Crisp

Day 6:
Breakfast: Cheesy Olive and Roasted Pepper Bread
Lunch: Shishito Peppers with Sour Cream Dipping Sauce
Snack: Cauliflower Buffalo Bites with Blue Cheese Dipping Sauce
Dinner: Fish Fillets with Lemon-Dill Sauce
Dessert: Air Fried Beignets

Day 7:
Breakfast: Cranberry Orange Muffins
Lunch: Herbed Shiitake Mushrooms
Snack: Sweet and Spicy Nuts
Dinner: Parmesan Pork Chops
Dessert: Nutmeg Butter Cookies

Chapter 1 Breakfast Recipes

Lemony Blueberry Muffins

Prep Time: 10 minutes | Cook Time: 20-25 minutes | Serves: 6

1¼ cups all-purpose flour
3 tablespoons granulated sugar
1 teaspoon baking powder
2 large eggs
3 tablespoons melted butter
1 tablespoon milk
1 tablespoon fresh lemon juice
½ cup fresh blueberries

1. Lightly coat 6 silicone muffin cups with vegetable oil. Set aside.
2. In a large mixing bowl, combine the all-purpose flour, sugar, and baking soda. Set aside.
3. In a separate small bowl, whisk together the eggs, butter, milk, and lemon juice. Add the egg mixture to the flour mixture and stir until just combined. Add the blueberries and let the batter sit for 5 minutes.
4. Spoon the batter into the muffin cups, about two-thirds full. Place the muffin cups on the sheet pan.
5. Select BAKE, set temperature to 350°F, and set time to 20 minutes. Press START/STOP to begin preheating.
6. When the unit has preheated, place the basket into the upper rails of the oven. Bake for 20 to 25 minutes, or until a toothpick inserted into the center of a muffin comes out clean.
7. Remove the sheet pan from the unit and let the muffins cool for about 5 minutes. Then transfer to a wire rack to cool completely.

Avocado and Egg Breakfast Bagel

Prep Time: 10 minutes | Cook Time: 5 minutes | Serves: 2

2 whole wheat bagels, halved
1 ripe avocado, mashed
2 boiled eggs, halved
½ teaspoon salt
¼ teaspoon black pepper
1 tablespoon lemon juice

1. Select Bagel, set the number of slices to 4, and set the shade level to your preference.
2. Place the bagel slices, cut-side up, on the wire rack into bottom rails. Press the START/STOP button to begin cooking. Cook for 5 minutes
3. Spread the mashed avocado onto each toasted bagel half. Top with the egg slices, salt, pepper, and a drizzle of lemon juice. Serve immediately for a nutritious breakfast.

Crispy Breakfast Quesadilla

Prep Time: 10 minutes | Cook Time: 6 minutes | Serves: 2

2 large flour tortillas
4 large eggs
½ cup shredded cheddar cheese
½ cup cooked bacon bits
½ cup diced bell peppers (red and green)
¼ teaspoon salt
¼ teaspoon black pepper
1 tablespoon butter, melted

1. Scramble the eggs in a pan and season with the salt and black pepper.
2. Lay one tortilla flat and sprinkle half of the cheese evenly over it.
3. Add the scrambled eggs, cooked bacon bits, and diced bell peppers.
4. Sprinkle the remaining cheese on top and cover with the second tortilla.
5. Brush the outside of the tortillas with melted butter. Place the quesadilla in the air fryer basket.
6. Select AIR FRY, set temperature to 375°F, and set time to 6 minutes. Press START/STOP to begin preheating.
7. When the unit has preheated, place the basket into the upper rails of the oven. Flip the quesadilla halfway through the cooking time.
8. Once the quesadilla is golden brown and crispy, remove from the unit, cut into wedges, and serve warm.

Cheesy Olive and Roasted Pepper Bread

Prep Time: 15 minutes | Cook Time: 7 minutes | Serves: 8

7-inch round bread boule
Olive oil
½ cup mayonnaise
2 tablespoons butter, melted
1 cup grated mozzarella or Fontina cheese
¼ cup grated Parmesan cheese
½ teaspoon dried oregano
½ cup black olives, sliced
½ cup green olives, sliced
½ cup coarsely chopped roasted red peppers
2 tablespoons minced red onion
Freshly ground black pepper

1. Cut the bread boule in half horizontally. If your bread boule has a rounded top, trim the top of the boule so that the top half will lie flat with the cut side facing up. Lightly brush both sides of the boule halves with olive oil.
2. Select Toast, set the number of bread slices to 2, and set the shade level to your preference.
3. Place the bread slices on the wire rack into bottom rails. Press the START/STOP button to begin cooking. Toast for 2 minutes.
4. Combine the mayonnaise, butter, mozzarella cheese, Parmesan cheese and dried oregano in a small bowl. Fold in the black and green olives, roasted red peppers and red onion and season with freshly ground black pepper. Spread the cheese mixture over the untoasted side of the bread, covering the entire surface.
5. Select Pizza, set temperature to 350°F, and set time to 5 minutes. Press START/STOP to begin preheating.
6. Place the bread on the wire rack. When the unit has preheated, place the wire rack into the bottom rails. Bake until the cheese is melted and browned.
7. Cut into slices and serve warm.

Jalapeño Popper Egg Cups

Prep Time: 10 minutes | Cook Time: 10 minutes | Serves: 2

4 large eggs
¼ cup chopped pickled jalapeños
2 ounces full-fat cream cheese
½ cup shredded sharp Cheddar cheese

1. In a medium bowl, beat the eggs, then pour into 4 silicone muffin cups.
2. In a large microwave-safe bowl, place the jalapeños, cream cheese, and Cheddar. Microwave for 30 seconds and stir. Take a spoonful, approximately ¼ of the mixture, and place it in the center of one of the egg cups. Repeat with the remaining mixture.
3. Place the egg cups in the air fryer basket.
4. Select AIR FRY, set temperature to 320°F, and set time to 10 minutes. Press START/STOP to begin preheating.
5. When the unit has preheated, place the basket into the upper rails of the oven.
6. When done, serve warm.

Egg-Loaded Potato Skins

Prep Time: 10 minutes | Cook Time: 55 minutes | Serves: 4

2 large russet potatoes
½ teaspoon olive oil
½ cup Gruyère cheese, shredded and divided
4 large eggs
¼ cup heavy (whipping) cream, divided
1 scallion, both white and green parts, finely chopped
Sea salt, for seasoning
Freshly ground black pepper, for seasoning

1. Prick the potatoes all over with a fork and rub with the olive oil. Place the potatoes in the air fry basket.
2. Select AIR FRY, set temperature to 400°F, and set time to 40 minutes. Press START/STOP to begin preheating.
3. When the unit has preheated, place the basket into the upper rails of the oven. The potatoes should be soft and tender, and the skin lightly browned. If not done, set the timer for 5 minutes more.
4. Take the potatoes out and set aside until cool enough to handle, about 10 minutes.
5. Cut the potatoes in half lengthwise and scoop out the flesh so that you have about ½-inch flesh and the intact skin. Place the potato halves in the air fryer basket and sprinkle 2 tablespoons of cheese in each skin. Crack an egg into each potato half and spoon 1 tablespoon of cream over each egg. Sprinkle with the scallion and lightly season with the salt and pepper.
6. Cook for 15 minutes until the egg whites are set, and the yolks are still runny. If the eggs need more time, set the timer for 3 to 5 minutes more. Serve.

Breakfast Calzone

Prep Time: 15 minutes | Cook Time: 15 minutes | Serves: 4

1½ cups shredded mozzarella cheese
½ cup all-purpose flour
1 ounce full-fat cream cheese
1 large whole egg
4 large eggs, scrambled
½ pound cooked breakfast sausage, crumbled
8 tablespoons shredded mild Cheddar cheese

1. In a large microwave-safe bowl, add the all-purpose flour, mozzarella, and cream cheese. Microwave for 1 minute. Stir until the mixture is smooth and forms a ball. Add the egg and stir until dough forms.
2. Arrange the dough between two sheets of parchment and roll out to ¼" thickness. Cut the dough into four rectangles.
3. Mix the scrambled eggs and cooked sausage together in a large bowl. Divide the mixture evenly among each piece of dough, placing it on the lower half of the rectangle. Sprinkle each with 2 tablespoons Cheddar.
4. Fold over the rectangle to cover the egg and meat mixture. Pinch, roll, or use a wet fork to close the edges completely.
5. Cut a piece of parchment to fit the air fryer basket and place the calzones onto the parchment.
6. Select AIR FRY, set temperature to 380°F, and set time to 15 minutes. Press START/STOP to begin preheating.
7. When the unit has preheated, place the basket into the upper rails of the oven. Flip the calzones halfway through the cooking time.
8. When done, the calzones should be golden in color. Serve immediately.

Cranberry Orange Muffins

Prep Time: 15 minutes | Cook Time: 25 minutes | Serves: 12

Nonstick cooking spray
2¼ cups all-purpose flour
¾ cup sugar
2 teaspoons baking powder
Finely grated zest and juice of 1 orange (about 2 teaspoons zest and ¼ cup juice)
½ teaspoon kosher salt
¼ teaspoon baking soda
10 tablespoons (1¼ sticks) unsalted butter, at room temperature, cut into ½-inch pieces
¼ cup whole milk
2 large eggs
1 teaspoon vanilla extract
1 cup dried cranberries

1. Coat 12 muffin cups with cooking spray.
2. Combine the flour, sugar, baking powder, orange zest, salt, baking soda, and butter in the bowl of a stand mixer with a paddle attachment (or use a hand mixer). Mix on low speed for about 2 minutes, until the butter has broken into very small clumps. The mixture will look powdery but hold together when pinched.
3. Add the milk, orange juice, eggs, and vanilla. Mix on low just until combined and very thick.
4. Stir in the cranberries.
5. Divide the batter evenly among the prepared muffin cups and place the muffin cups on the sheet pan, working in batches.
6. Select BAKE, set temperature to 350°F, and set time to 25 minutes. Press START/STOP to begin preheating.
7. When the unit has preheated, place the sheet pan on wire rack into the bottom rails. Bake until the muffins are puffed, golden brown, and firm to the touch, rotating the muffin cups after 15 minutes if cooking unevenly.

Ham and Egg Cups

Prep Time: 10 minutes | Cook Time: 15 minutes | Serves: 6

6 thin slices ham
6 large eggs
Kosher salt
Freshly ground black pepper
2 tablespoons finely grated Parmesan cheese

1. Spray 6 muffin cups with cooking spray. Press a slice of ham into each cup, smoothing out the sides as much as possible. The ham should extend over the top of the cup by ¼ to ½ inch. Crack an egg into each cup and season with the salt and pepper. Top each yolk with 1 teaspoon of the cheese. Place the muffin cups in the air fryer basket.
2. Select AIR FRY, set temperature to 375°F, and set time to 5 minutes. Press START/STOP to begin preheating.
3. When the unit has preheated, place the basket into the upper rails of the oven. Cook for 5 minutes, then slide out the rail, and check the eggs. They should just be starting to firm up and turn opaque. Rotate the muffin cups if the eggs are cooking unevenly.
4. Cook for another 5 minutes and check again; if the egg whites are cooked through, remove the sheet pan from the unit. The total cook time is about 12 minutes for fully cooked whites and runny yolks; if you prefer the yolks more done, cook for an additional minute or two.
5. When the eggs are cooked as desired, remove the muffin cups and let cool for a couple of minutes. Run a thin knife around the ham and use a spoon to remove the cups.

Ham and Cheese Pastries

Prep Time: 10 minutes | Cook Time: 20 minutes | Serves: 4

¾ cup diced ham
½ cup shredded Gruyère or other Swiss-style cheese
2 tablespoons cream cheese, softened
1 tablespoon Dijon mustard
1 sheet frozen puff pastry, thawed
1 large egg, beaten
2 tablespoons finely grated Parmesan cheese

1. Line the sheet pan with parchment paper.
2. In a medium bowl, stir together the ham, shredded cheese, cream cheese, and mustard.
3. Lightly flour a cutting board. Unfold the puff pastry sheet onto the board. Gently roll the dough with a rolling pin to smooth out the folds, sealing any tears. Cut the dough into four squares.
4. Scoop a quarter of the ham mixture into the center of each puff pastry square, then spread the ham sauce evenly in a triangle over half the pastry, leaving a ½-inch border around the edges. Fold the pastry diagonally over the filling to form triangles. Using a fork, crimp the edges to seal them. Arrange the pastries on the prepared sheet pan, spacing them evenly.
5. Cut two or three small slits into the top of each turnover. Brush with the egg and sprinkle the Parmesan on top.
6. Select BAKE, set temperature to 350°F, and set time to 10 minutes. Press START/STOP to begin preheating.
7. When the unit has preheated, place the sheet pan on wire rack into the bottom rails. Bake for 10 to 12 minutes, then remove from the unit. Check the pastries; if they are browning unevenly, flip the pastries. Return the sheet pan to the unit and continue baking for another 10 minutes, or until the turnovers are golden brown.
8. Let cool for about 10 minutes before serving (the filling will be very hot).

Cheesy Bell Pepper Eggs

Prep Time: 10 minutes | Cook Time: 15 minutes | Serves: 4

4 medium green bell peppers
3 ounces cooked ham, chopped
¼ medium onion, peeled and chopped
8 large eggs
1 cup mild Cheddar cheese

1. Cut the tops off each bell pepper. Remove the seeds and the white membranes with a small knife. Place the ham and onion into each pepper.
2. Crack 2 eggs into each pepper. Top with ¼ cup cheese per pepper. Place in the air fryer basket.
3. Select AIR FRY, set temperature to 390°F, and set time to 15 minutes. Press START/STOP to begin preheating.
4. When the unit has preheated, place the basket into the upper rails of the oven.
5. When fully cooked, peppers will be tender and eggs will be firm. Serve immediately.

Sausage Cheddar Scones

Prep Time: 15 minutes | Cook Time: 15 minutes | Serves: 6

1½ cups all-purpose flour
2 teaspoons baking powder
½ teaspoon kosher salt
3 tablespoons unsalted butter, very cold
1 cup coarsely grated sharp Cheddar cheese
2 or 3 scallions, finely chopped (about ¼ cup)
8 ounces breakfast sausage, cooked and coarsely chopped
1 large egg, beaten, divided
½ cup heavy (whipping) cream

1. Line the sheet pan with parchment paper.
2. In a large bowl, whisk together the flour, baking powder, and salt. Using the large holes of a cheese grater, grate the butter into the flour mixture and stir to combine. Mix in the cheese, scallions, and sausage.
3. Pour 1 tablespoon of the beaten egg into a small bowl and set aside. Whisk the cream into the remaining egg. Add the egg mixture to the flour and butter mixture. The dough should hold together but be shaggy rather than moist.
4. Transfer the dough to a lightly floured work surface. Gather it together into a rectangle. Fold the dough into thirds and press together. Repeat.
5. Form the dough into a smooth 6-inch disk. Cut the disk into 6 wedges, and carefully transfer them to the prepared sheet pan, working in batches if necessary. Brush the scones with the reserved egg.
6. Select BAKE, set temperature to 400°F, and set time to 15 minutes. Press START/STOP to begin preheating.
7. When the unit has preheated, place the sheet pan on wire rack into the bottom rails. Bake for 15 to 18 minutes, until golden brown, flipping halfway through if they're browning unevenly.
8. Cool on the sheet pan for about 10 minutes. Serve warm or at room temperature.

French Toast Casserole

Prep Time: 10 minutes | Cook Time: 30–35 minutes | Serves: 6

1 loaf (12-ounce) of day-old French bread, cut into 1-inch cubes
6 large eggs
1½ cups whole milk
½ cup heavy cream
⅓ cup granulated sugar
¼ cup brown sugar
2 teaspoons vanilla extract
1 teaspoon ground cinnamon
¼ teaspoon ground nutmeg
Pinch of salt
4 tablespoons unsalted butter, melted
Powdered sugar, for dusting (optional)
Maple syrup, for serving

1. Lightly grease a baking dish that fits the unit with nonstick cooking spray or butter.
2. Place the cubed bread evenly in the prepared baking dish.
3. In a large bowl, whisk together the eggs, milk, heavy cream, granulated sugar, brown sugar, cinnamon, vanilla extract, nutmeg, and salt until smooth.
4. Pour the custard mixture evenly over the bread cubes. Gently press the bread down to help it soak up the liquid. Cover and refrigerate for at least 1 hour or overnight for best results.
5. Select BAKE, set temperature to 350°F, and set time to 30 minutes. Press START/STOP to begin preheating.
6. When the unit has preheated, place the baking dish on wire rack into the bottom rails. Bake for 30–35 minutes or until the top is golden brown and the center is set. If the top browns too quickly, loosely cover it with foil.
7. Let the casserole cool for 5 minutes. Drizzle with the melted butter, dust with the powdered sugar if desired, and serve warm with maple syrup.

Sausage Cheese Balls

Prep Time: 10 minutes | Cook Time: 12 minutes | Serves: 4

1 pound pork breakfast sausage
½ cup shredded Cheddar cheese
1 ounce full-fat cream cheese, softened
1 large egg

1. Mix all ingredients in a large bowl. Form into sixteen (1") balls. Place the balls in the air fryer basket.
2. Select AIR FRY, set temperature to 400°F, and set time to 12 minutes. Press START/STOP to begin preheating.
3. When the unit has preheated, place the basket on the top rails while sliding in the sheet pan and wire rack on the bottom rails.
4. Flip the meatballs two or three times during cooking. Sausage balls will be browned on the outside and have an internal temperature of at least 145°F when completely cooked. Serve warm.

Cinnamon Rolls with Cream Cheese Glaze

Prep Time: 10 minutes | Cook Time: 8 minutes | Serves: 8

1 pound frozen bread dough, thawed
¼ cup butter, melted and cooled
¾ cup brown sugar
1½ tablespoons ground cinnamon
Cream Cheese Glaze:
4 ounces cream cheese, softened
2 tablespoons butter, softened
1¼ cups powdered sugar
½ teaspoon vanilla

1. Allow the bread dough to come to room temperature on the counter. On a lightly floured surface, roll the dough into a 13-inch by 11-inch rectangle. Arrange the rectangle so the 13-inch side is facing you. Brush the melted butter all over the dough, leaving a 1-inch border uncovered along the edge farthest away from you.
2. In a small bowl, mix the brown sugar and cinnamon. Sprinkle the mixture evenly over the buttered dough, keeping the 1-inch border uncovered. Roll the dough into a log starting with the edge closest to you. Roll the dough tightly, making sure to roll evenly and push out any air pockets. When you get to the uncovered edge of the dough, press the dough onto the roll to seal it together.
3. Cut the log into 8 pieces slicing slowly with a sawing motion so you don't flatten the dough. Turn the slices on their sides and cover with a clean kitchen towel. Allow the rolls to sit in the warmest part of your kitchen for 1½ to 2 hours to rise.
4. Working in batches if necessary, place the rolls in the air fryer basket.
5. Select AIR FRY, set temperature to 350°F, and set time to 5 minutes. Press START/STOP to begin preheating.
6. When the unit has preheated, place the basket into the upper rails of the oven.
7. Turn the rolls over and cook for another 4 minutes. Repeat with the remaining rolls.
8. Allow the rolls to cool for a couple of minutes before glazing. Top the warm cinnamon rolls with large dollops of cream cheese glaze, allowing some of the glaze to drip down the side of the rolls. Serve warm and enjoy!

To make the glaze:
1. Add the cream cheese and butter in a microwave-safe bowl. Soften in the microwave for 30 seconds at a time until it is easy to stir. Gradually add the powdered sugar and stir to combine. Add the vanilla extract and whisk until smooth. Set aside.

Cherry Tomato Avocado Toast

Prep Time: 5 minutes | Cook Time: 3 minutes | Serves: 2

4 slices whole-grain bread
1 ripe avocado, mashed
½ cup cherry tomatoes, halved
½ teaspoon red pepper flakes
1 tablespoon olive oil
Salt and pepper to taste

1. Select Toast, set the number of bread slices to 4, and set the shade level to your preference.
2. Place the bread slices on the wire rack into bottom rails. Press the START/STOP button to begin cooking. Toast for 3 minutes.
3. Spread the mashed avocado over the toast. Top with the cherry tomatoes, red pepper flakes, and a drizzle of olive oil. Serve immediately with a sprinkle of salt and pepper.

Chapter 2 Vegetable and Side Recipes

Zucchini Salad with Feta and Parsley

Prep Time: 10 minutes | Cook Time: 5-7 minutes | Serves: 4

2 medium zucchini, thinly sliced
5 tablespoons olive oil, divided
¼ cup chopped fresh parsley
2 tablespoons chopped fresh mint
Zest and juice of ½ lemon
1 clove garlic, minced
¼ cup crumbled feta cheese
Freshly ground black pepper

1. In a large bowl, toss the zucchini slices with 1 tablespoon olive oil.
2. Working in batches if necessary, place the zucchini slices in an even layer on the sheet pan.
3. Select AIR ROAST, set temperature to 400°F, and set time to 5 minutes. Press START/STOP to begin preheating.
4. When the unit has preheated, place the sheet pan on the wire rack into the bottom rails. Roast for 5 to 7 minutes until soft and lightly browned on each side, tossing the slices halfway through the cooking time.
5. Meanwhile, in a small bowl, combine the remaining 4 tablespoons olive oil, parsley, mint, lemon zest, lemon juice, and garlic.
6. Arrange the zucchini on a plate and drizzle with the dressing. Sprinkle the feta and black pepper on top. Serve warm or at room temperature.

Mini Hasselback Potatoes

Prep Time: 10 minutes | Cook Time: 25 minutes | Serves: 4-5

1½ pounds baby Yukon Gold potatoes (about 10)
5 tablespoons butter, cut into very thin slices
Salt and freshly ground black pepper
1 tablespoon vegetable oil
¼ cup grated Parmesan cheese (optional)
Chopped fresh parsley or chives

1. Make six to eight deep vertical slits across the top of each potato about three quarters of the way down. Make sure the slits are deep enough to allow the slices to spread apart a little, but don't cut all the way through the potato. Place a thin slice of butter between each of the slices and season generously with salt and pepper.
2. Transfer the potatoes to the air fryer basket. Pack them in next to each other. It's alright if some of the potatoes sit on top or rest on another potato.
3. Select AIR FRY, set temperature to 400°F, and set time to 20 minutes. Press START/STOP to begin preheating.
4. When the unit has preheated, place the basket into the upper rails of the oven.
5. Spray or brush the potatoes with a little vegetable oil and sprinkle the Parmesan cheese on top (if using). Cook for an additional 5 minutes.
6. Garnish with the chopped parsley or chives and serve hot.

Lemon Thyme Asparagus

Prep Time: 5 minutes | Cook Time: 4-8 minutes | Serves: 4

1 pound asparagus, woody ends trimmed off
1 tablespoon avocado oil
½ teaspoon dried thyme or ½ tablespoon chopped fresh thyme
Sea salt
Freshly ground black pepper
2 ounces goat cheese, crumbled
Zest and juice of 1 lemon
Flaky sea salt, for serving (optional)

1. In a medium bowl, toss together the asparagus, avocado oil, and thyme, and season with the sea salt and pepper.
2. Place the asparagus on the sheet pan in a single layer.
3. Select AIR ROAST, set temperature to 400°F, and set time to 4 minutes. Press START/STOP to begin preheating.
4. When the unit has preheated, place the sheet pan on the wire rack into the bottom rails. Cook for 4 to 8 minutes, to your desired doneness.
5. Transfer to a serving platter. Top with the goat cheese, lemon zest, and lemon juice. If desired, season with a pinch of flaky salt.

Cauliflower Steak with Gremolata

Prep Time: 10 minutes | Cook Time: 20-25 minutes | Serves: 4

2 tablespoons olive oil
1 tablespoon Italian seasoning
1 large head cauliflower, outer leaves removed and sliced lengthwise through the core into thick "steaks"
Salt and freshly ground black pepper
¼ cup Parmesan cheese

Gremolata:
1 bunch Italian parsley (about 1 cup packed)
2 cloves garlic
Zest of 1 small lemon, plus 1–2 teaspoons lemon juice
½ cup olive oil
Salt and pepper to taste

1. In a small bowl, combine the olive oil and Italian seasoning. Brush both sides of each cauliflower steak generously with the oil. Season to taste with the salt and black pepper.
2. Working in batches if necessary, arrange the cauliflower in a single layer on the sheet pan.
3. Select AIR ROAST, set temperature to 400°F, and set time to 15 minutes. Press START/STOP to begin preheating.
4. When the unit has preheated, place the sheet pan on the wire rack into the bottom rails.
5. Cook for 15 to 20 minutes until the cauliflower is tender and the edges begin to brown, turning the "steaks" halfway through the cooking time. Sprinkle with the Parmesan and cook for 5 minutes longer.

To make the gremolata:
1. In a food processor fitted with a metal blade, combine the parsley, garlic, and lemon zest and juice. With the motor running, add the olive oil in a steady stream until the mixture forms a bright green sauce. Season to taste with the salt and black pepper.
2. Serve the cauliflower steaks with the gremolata spooned over the top.

Ratatouille Vegetables

Prep Time: 10 minutes | Cook Time: 15 minutes | Serves: 2-4

1 baby or Japanese eggplant, cut into 1½-inch cubes
1 red pepper, cut into 1-inch chunks
1 yellow pepper, cut into 1-inch chunks
1 zucchini, cut into 1-inch chunks
1 clove garlic, minced
½ teaspoon dried basil
1 tablespoon olive oil
Salt and freshly ground black pepper
¼ cup sliced sun-dried tomatoes in oil
2 tablespoons chopped fresh basil

1. Toss the eggplant, peppers, and zucchini with the garlic, dried basil, olive oil, salt, and freshly ground black pepper in a large bowl. Transfer to the sheet pan.
2. Select AIR ROAST, set temperature to 400°F, and set time to 15 minutes. Press START/STOP to begin preheating.
3. When the unit has preheated, place the sheet pan on the wire rack into the bottom rails. Toss the vegetables a few times during the cooking process to redistribute the ingredients.
4. As soon as the vegetables are tender, toss them with the sliced sun-dried tomatoes and fresh basil and serve.

Healthy Bell Pepper Salad

Prep Time: 15 minutes | Cook Time: 5 minutes | Serves: 4

4 bell peppers, a combination of red, yellow, and orange
3 tablespoons chopped fresh flat-leaf parsley
2 small garlic cloves, minced
4 teaspoons sherry vinegar
½ teaspoon Dijon mustard
¼ cup extra-virgin olive oil
3 cups bitter greens, such as arugula, watercress, or a spring mix
3 tablespoons drained capers
2 tablespoons crumbled ricotta salata or feta cheese

1. Remove the stems from the peppers and cut each into 2 or 3 flat pieces. Remove the seeds and ribs. Place the peppers in the air fryer basket, skin-side up.
2. Select AIR FRY, set temperature to 400°F, and set time to 4 minutes. Press START/STOP to begin preheating.
3. When the unit has preheated, place the basket into the upper rails of the oven. Cook for 4 to 5 minutes, until the skins are almost completely charred.
4. Transfer the pieces to a glass or metal bowl and pour any pan juices over them. Cover the bowl with a plate (or plastic wrap or aluminum foil). Let the peppers steam and cool for 10 minutes.
5. Remove the peppers from the bowl. Drain any accumulated liquid into a separate small bowl. Peel the burned skins off the peppers. Cut the peppers into ½-inch strips and return them to their original bowl. Add the parsley.
6. Add the garlic, vinegar, and mustard to the reserved liquid from the peppers and stir until smooth. Drizzle in the oil while continuing to stir. Pour the dressing over the peppers. Cover and refrigerate for at least 1 hour and up to 2 days.
7. Divide the greens among 6 plates. Drape the pepper strips over the greens, drizzle with a little vinaigrette, and sprinkle with the capers. Top with the cheese and serve.

Shishito Peppers with Sour Cream Dipping Sauce

Prep Time: 5 minutes | Cook Time: 6 minutes | Serves: 4

For the Dipping Sauce:
1 cup sour cream
2 tablespoons fresh lemon juice
1 clove garlic, minced
1 green onion (white and green parts), finely chopped

For the Peppers:
8 ounces shishito peppers
1 tablespoon vegetable oil
1 teaspoon toasted sesame oil
Kosher salt and black pepper
¼ to ½ teaspoon red pepper flakes (optional)
½ teaspoon toasted sesame seeds

To make the dipping sauce:
1. In a small bowl, stir all the ingredients to combine. Cover and refrigerate until serving time.

To make the peppers:
1. In a medium bowl, toss the peppers with the vegetable oil. Place the peppers on the sheet pan.
2. Select AIR ROAST, set temperature to 400°F, and set time to 6 minutes. Press START/STOP to begin preheating.
3. When the unit has preheated, place the sheet pan on the wire rack into the bottom rails. Roast until peppers are lightly charred in spots, flipping the peppers halfway through the cooking time.
4. Transfer the peppers to a serving bowl, drizzle with the sesame oil, and toss to coat. Season to taste with the salt and pepper. Sprinkle with the red pepper, if using, and the sesame seeds and toss again.
5. Serve immediately with the dipping sauce.

Herbed Shiitake Mushrooms

Prep Time: 10 minutes | Cook Time: 5 minutes | Serves: 4

8 ounces shiitake mushrooms, stems removed and caps roughly chopped
1 tablespoon olive oil
½ teaspoon salt
Freshly ground black pepper
1 teaspoon chopped fresh thyme leaves
1 teaspoon chopped fresh oregano
1 tablespoon chopped fresh parsley

1. Toss the mushrooms with the olive oil, salt, pepper, thyme, and oregano. Place the mushrooms on the sheet pan.
2. Select AIR ROAST, set temperature to 400°F, and set time to 5 minutes. Press START/STOP to begin preheating.
3. When the unit has preheated, place the sheet pan on the wire rack into the bottom rails. Toss the mushrooms once or twice during the cooking process. The mushrooms will still be somewhat chewy with a meaty texture. If you'd like them a little more tender, add a couple of minutes to this cooking time.
4. Once cooked, add the parsley to the mushrooms and toss. Season again to taste and serve.

Roasted Rosemary Potatoes

Prep Time: 5 minutes | Cook Time: 30-35 minutes | Serves: 4-6

2 pounds small potatoes (such as red- or white-skinned new potatoes or Yukon golds), halved
2 tablespoons olive oil
2 tablespoons unsalted butter, melted
2 tablespoons chopped fresh rosemary leaves
1 teaspoon kosher salt

1. In a bowl, toss the potatoes with the oil, melted butter, rosemary, and salt until thoroughly coated. Transfer to the sheet pan.
2. Select AIR ROAST, set temperature to 400°F, and set time to 30 minutes. Press START/STOP to begin preheating.
3. When the unit has preheated, place the sheet pan on the wire rack into the bottom rails. Roast for 30 to 35 minutes, stirring occasionally, until golden brown and crispy on the outside and tender in the middle. Serve immediately.

Carrots with Cumin-Orange Vinaigrette

Prep Time: 10 minutes | Cook Time: 30 minutes | Serves: 4

2 pounds carrots
2 tablespoons vegetable oil
2 teaspoons kosher salt, divided
½ teaspoon cumin seeds
2 tablespoons extra-virgin olive oil
2 tablespoons orange juice
2 tablespoons chopped fresh mint

1. Peel the carrots and cut into 3-inch pieces. The pieces should be about ½-inch thick (about the size of a finger), so halve them lengthwise if medium-size or quarter them if large. Put the carrots on the sheet pan and drizzle with the vegetable oil and 1 teaspoon of salt. Toss to coat.
2. Select AIR ROAST, set temperature to 400°F, and set time to 15 minutes. Press START/STOP to begin preheating.
3. When the unit has preheated, place the sheet pan on the wire rack into the bottom rails.
4. Toss and cook for another 15 to 20 minutes, or until tender and browned in spots.
5. Meanwhile, crush the cumin seeds with a heavy skillet or a mortar and pestle, or pulse briefly in a spice grinder until broken up but not powdery. When the carrots are done, turn off the oven. Sprinkle the cumin seeds over the carrots and return them to the unit for 30 to 60 seconds, just until the cumin is fragrant.
6. In a small bowl, whisk together the olive oil, orange juice, and remaining 1 teaspoon of salt. Drizzle the vinaigrette over the carrots and sprinkle with the mint. Serve warm or at room temperature.

Veggie Burgers

Prep Time: 10 minutes | Cook Time: 12 minutes | Serves: 4

8 ounces cremini mushrooms
2 large egg yolks
½ medium zucchini, trimmed and chopped
¼ cup peeled and chopped yellow onion
1 clove garlic, peeled and finely minced
½ teaspoon salt
¼ teaspoon ground black pepper

1. Place all ingredients into a food processor and pulse twenty times until finely chopped and combined.
2. Separate the mixture into four equal sections and press each into a burger shape. Place the burgers in the air fryer basket.
3. Select AIR FRY, set temperature to 375°F, and set time to 12 minutes. Press START/STOP to begin preheating.
4. When the unit has preheated, place the basket into the upper rails of the oven. Turn the burgers halfway through cooking. Burgers will be browned and firm when done.
5. Place the burgers on a large plate and let cool 5 minutes before serving.

Sweet and Sour Brussels Sprouts

Prep Time: 10 minutes | Cook Time: 30 minutes | Serves: 4

2 pounds Brussels sprouts
2 to 3 tablespoons vegetable oil
1 teaspoon kosher salt
¼ cup balsamic vinegar
2 tablespoons brown sugar
Freshly ground black pepper

1. Trim the ends of the Brussels sprouts and peel off any damaged outer leaves. Cut the sprouts in half through the stem end.
2. Put the sprouts on the sheet pan and drizzle with the oil, stirring to coat evenly. Sprinkle with the salt. Arrange the sprouts cut-side down.
3. Select AIR ROAST, set temperature to 375°F, and set time to 20 minutes. Press START/STOP to begin preheating.
4. When the unit has preheated, place the sheet pan on the wire rack into the bottom rails. Cook just until crisp-tender.
5. Meanwhile, stir together the balsamic vinegar, brown sugar, and pepper until the sugar dissolves.
6. Remove the sprouts from the unit, pour the balsamic mixture over them, and toss to coat. Return the sheet pan to the unit and cook for another 10 minutes, until tender, browned, and glazed.

| Chapter 2 Vegetable and Side Recipes

Sesame Green Beans

Prep Time: 5 minutes | Cook Time: 8 minutes | Serves: 4

1 pound green beans, stems trimmed
1 tablespoon olive oil
1 teaspoon sesame oil
1 tablespoon sesame seeds
Pinch sea salt

1. In a large bowl, toss the green beans, olive oil, and sesame oil. Spread the beans on the sheet pan.
2. Select AIR ROAST, set temperature to 350°F, and set time to 8 minutes. Press START/STOP to begin preheating.
3. When the unit has preheated, place the sheet pan on the wire rack into the bottom rails. Toss the beans halfway through the cooking time. The beans should be lightly golden and fragrant.
4. Transfer the beans to a serving plate and serve topped with the sesame seeds and seasoned with the salt.

Spicy Vegetable and Tofu

Prep Time: 10 minutes | Cook Time: 17-19 minutes | Serves: 4-6

4 teaspoons canola oil, divided
2 tablespoons rice wine vinegar
1 tablespoon sriracha chili sauce
¼ cup soy sauce
½ teaspoon toasted sesame oil
1 teaspoon minced garlic
1 tablespoon minced fresh ginger
8 ounces extra firm tofu
½ cup vegetable stock or water
1 tablespoon honey
1 tablespoon cornstarch
½ red onion, chopped
1 red or yellow bell pepper, chopped
1 cup green beans, cut into 2-inch lengths
4 ounces mushrooms, sliced
2 scallions, sliced
2 tablespoons fresh cilantro leaves
2 teaspoons toasted sesame seeds

1. Combine 1 tablespoon of the oil, vinegar, soy sauce, sriracha sauce, sesame oil, garlic, and ginger in a small bowl. Cut the tofu into bite-sized cubes and toss the tofu in with the marinade while you prepare the other vegetables. When you are ready to start cooking, remove the tofu from the marinade and set it aside. Add the water, honey, and cornstarch to the marinade and bring to a simmer on the stovetop, just until the sauce thickens. Set the sauce aside.
2. Toss the onion, pepper, green beans, and mushrooms in a bowl with a little canola oil and season with the salt. Transfer to the sheet pan.
3. Select AIR ROAST, set temperature to 400°F, and set time to 10 minutes. Press START/STOP to begin preheating.
4. When the unit has preheated, place the sheet pan on the wire rack into the bottom rails. Roast for 10 to 12 minutes, tossing the vegetables every few minutes.
5. When the vegetables are cooked to your preferred doneness, remove them from the sheet pan and set aside.
6. Add the tofu to the sheet pan and cook at 400°F for 6 minutes, tossing a few times during the cooking process. Add the vegetables back to the sheet pan and cook for another minute.
7. Transfer the vegetables and tofu to a large bowl, add the scallions and cilantro leaves and toss with the sauce. Serve over rice with the sesame seeds sprinkled on top.

Parsnip Fries with Romesco Sauce

Prep Time: 10 minutes | Cook Time: 22-24 minutes | Serves: 2

3 parsnips, peeled and cut into long strips
2 teaspoons olive oil
Salt and freshly ground black pepper
Romesco Sauce:
1 red bell pepper, halved and seeded
1 (1-inch) thick slice of Italian bread, torn into pieces (about 1 to 1½ cups)
1 cup almonds, toasted
Olive oil
½ Jalapeño pepper, seeded
1 tablespoon fresh parsley leaves
1 clove garlic
2 Roma tomatoes, peeled and seeded (or ⅓ cup canned crushed tomatoes)
1 tablespoon red wine vinegar
¼ teaspoon smoked paprika
½ teaspoon salt
¾ cup olive oil

1. Place the red pepper halves, cut side down, in the air fryer basket.
2. Select AIR FRY, set temperature to 400°F, and set time to 8 minutes. Press START/STOP to begin preheating.
3. When the unit has preheated, place the basket into the upper rails of the oven. Cook for 8 to 10 minutes, or until the skin turns black all over.
4. Remove the pepper from the basket and let it cool. When it is cool enough to handle, peel the pepper.
5. Toss the torn bread and almonds with a little olive oil, place on the air fryer basket lined with parchment paper, air fry for 4 minutes, tossing the mixture a couple times throughout the cooking time.
6. When the bread and almonds are nicely cooked, remove them from the basket and let them cool for just a minute or two.
7. Combine the toasted bread, almonds, parsley, garlic, cooked red pepper, Jalapeño pepper, tomatoes, vinegar, smoked paprika, and salt in a food processor or blender. Process until smooth. With the processor running, add the olive oil through the feed tube until the sauce comes together in a smooth paste that is barely pourable.
8. Toss the parsnip strips with the olive oil, salt, and freshly ground black pepper, place in the air fryer basket, and air fry at 400°F for 10 minutes, tossing the strips a couple times during the cooking process so they brown and cook evenly.
9. Serve the parsnip fries warm with the romesco sauce to dip into.

Cheesy Broccoli Sticks

Prep Time: 10 minutes | Cook Time: 16 minutes | Serves: 2

1 (10-ounce) steamer bag broccoli florets, cooked according to package instructions
1 large egg
1 ounce Parmesan 100% cheese crisps, finely ground
½ cup shredded sharp Cheddar cheese
½ teaspoon salt
½ cup ranch dressing

1. Let the cooked broccoli cool for 5 minutes, then place into a food processor with the egg, cheese crisps, Cheddar, and salt. Process on low for 30 seconds until all ingredients are combined and begin to stick together.
2. Cut a sheet of parchment paper to fit the air fryer basket. Take one scoop of mixture, about 3 tablespoons, and roll into a 4" stick shape, pressing down gently to flatten the top. Place the stick on the ungreased parchment. Repeat with the remaining mixture to form eight sticks.
3. Select AIR FRY, set temperature to 350°F, and set time to 16 minutes. Press START/STOP to begin preheating.
4. When the unit has preheated, place the basket into the upper rails of the oven. Turn the sticks halfway through cooking. Sticks will be golden brown when done.
5. Serve warm with the ranch dressing on the side for dipping.

Chapter 3 Snack and Appetizer Recipes

Dry Rub Chicken Wings

Prep Time: 10 minutes | Cook Time: 35-40 minutes | Serves: 4

1 tablespoon paprika
1 tablespoon granulated sugar
½ teaspoon dried oregano
½ teaspoon garlic powder
½ teaspoon freshly ground black pepper
½ teaspoon cayenne
1 pound chicken wings, tips removed

1. In a large bowl, combine the paprika, sugar, oregano, garlic powder, black pepper, and cayenne. Add the chicken wings and toss until thoroughly coated. Cover and refrigerate for at least 1 hour or up to 8 hours.
2. Arrange the wings in a single layer in the air fryer basket. Spray lightly with olive oil.
3. Flip the unit down to the horizontal position and push the lever back to the lock position.
4. Select AIR FRY, set temperature to 400°F, and set time to 35 minutes. Press START/STOP to begin preheating.
5. When the unit has preheated, place the basket on the top rails while sliding in the sheet pan and wire rack on the bottom rails. Cook for 35 to 40 minutes until crispy and browned and a thermometer inserted into the thickest part registers 165°F, turning the wings halfway through the cooking time.

Crispy Parmesan Artichokes

Prep Time: 10 minutes | Cook Time: 10 minutes | Serves: 4

2 medium artichokes, trimmed and quartered, center removed
2 tablespoons coconut oil
1 large egg, beaten
½ cup grated Parmesan cheese
¼ cup all-purpose flour
½ teaspoon crushed red pepper flakes

1. In a large bowl, toss the artichokes in the coconut oil and then dip each piece into the egg.
2. Mix the Parmesan and all-purpose flour in a large bowl. Add the artichoke pieces and toss to cover as completely as possible, sprinkle with the pepper flakes. Transfer to the air fryer basket.
3. Select AIR FRY, set temperature to 350°F, and set time to 10 minutes. Press START/STOP to begin preheating.
4. When the unit has preheated, place the basket into the upper rails of the oven. Toss the pieces two times during cooking.
5. When done, serve warm.

Bacon-Wrapped Jalapeño Poppers

Prep Time: 10 minutes | Cook Time: 15-20 minutes | Serves: 4

4 ounces cream cheese, softened
1 tablespoon hot sauce
1 teaspoon garlic powder
8 jalapeño peppers, halved lengthwise and seeded
8 slices reduced-sodium bacon, cut in half

1. In a small bowl, combine the cream cheese, hot sauce, and garlic powder.
2. Fill the pepper halves with equal amounts of the cream cheese mixture and wrap each pepper tightly with a half piece of bacon to enclose the ingredients. For best results, make sure the ends of the bacon are on the bottom of the peppers.
3. Arrange the peppers cut-side up in a single layer in the air fryer basket.
4. Select AIR FRY, set temperature to 350°F, and set time to 15 minutes. Press START/STOP to begin preheating.
5. When the unit has preheated, place the basket on the top rails while sliding in the sheet pan and wire rack on the bottom rails. Air fry for 15 to 20 minutes until the peppers are softened and the bacon is crisp. Let cool slightly before serving.

Mozzarella Sticks

Prep Time: 15 minutes | Cook Time: 8–10 minutes | Serves: 4

12 mozzarella cheese sticks (string cheese), halved
1 cup all-purpose flour
2 large eggs, beaten
2 tablespoons milk
1½ cups Italian-style breadcrumbs
½ cup grated Parmesan cheese
1 teaspoon garlic powder
1 teaspoon dried oregano
½ teaspoon paprika
Nonstick cooking spray or olive oil spray
Marinara sauce, for dipping

1. Cut each mozzarella stick in half to make 24 pieces. Place them on a baking sheet and freeze for at least 1 hour to prevent melting during cooking.
2. Set up the dredging station. In the first bowl, place the flour. In the second bowl, whisk together the eggs and milk. In the third bowl, combine breadcrumbs, Parmesan cheese, garlic powder, oregano, and paprika.
3. Remove the frozen mozzarella sticks from the freezer. Dip each stick first in flour (shaking off excess), then in the egg mixture, and finally coat thoroughly with the breadcrumb mixture. For an extra crispy layer, repeat the egg and breadcrumb steps.
4. Select AIR FRY, set temperature to 400°F, and set time to 8 minutes. Press START/STOP to begin preheating.
5. Lightly spray the air fryer basket with nonstick cooking spray. Arrange the coated mozzarella sticks in a single layer, leaving space between them. Lightly spray the sticks with oil to promote browning.
6. When the unit has preheated, place the basket into the upper rails of the oven. Air fry for 4–5 minutes, then flip the sticks and spray lightly again. Continue cooking for another 3–4 minutes, until golden brown and crispy.
7. Remove the mozzarella sticks from the unit and let them cool for 1–2 minutes. Serve warm with the marinara sauce for dipping.

Crispy Nacho Avocado Fries

Prep Time: 10 minutes | Cook Time: 15 minutes | Serves: 6

3 firm, barely ripe avocados, halved, peeled, and pitted
2 cups pork dust (or powdered Parmesan cheese for vegetarian)
2 teaspoons fine sea salt
2 teaspoons ground black pepper
2 teaspoons ground cumin
1 teaspoon chili powder
1 teaspoon paprika
½ teaspoon garlic powder
½ teaspoon onion powder
2 large eggs
Salsa, for serving (optional)
Fresh chopped cilantro leaves, for garnish (optional)

1. Spray the air fryer basket with avocado oil.
2. Slice the avocados into thick-cut french fry shapes.
3. In a bowl, mix together the pork dust, salt, pepper, and seasonings.
4. In a separate shallow bowl, beat the eggs.
5. Dip the avocado fries into the beaten eggs and shake off any excess, then dip them into the pork dust mixture. Use your hands to press the breading into each fry.
6. Spray the fries with avocado oil and place them in the basket in a single layer, leaving space between them. If there are too many fries to fit in a single layer, work in batches.
7. Select AIR FRY, set temperature to 400°F, and set time to 13 minutes. Press START/STOP to begin preheating.
8. When the unit has preheated, place the basket into the upper rails of the oven. Cook for 13 to 15 minutes, until golden brown, flipping after 5 minutes.
9. Serve with the salsa, if desired, and garnish with the fresh chopped cilantro, if desired. Store leftovers in an airtight container in the fridge for up to 5 days. Reheat in the preheated 400°F unit for 3 minutes, or until heated through.

Smoked Salmon & Cream Cheese Bagel

Prep Time: 10 minutes | Cook Time: 5 minutes | Serves: 2

2 sesame bagels, halved
½ cup cream cheese
4 ounces smoked salmon
1 tablespoon capers
2 slices red onion
1 teaspoon fresh dill

1. Select Bagel, set the number of slices to 4, and set the shade level to your preference.
2. Place the bagel slices, cut-side up, on the wire rack into bottom rails. Press the START/STOP button to begin cooking. Cook for 5 minutes.
3. Spread the cream cheese on the bagels and layer with the smoked salmon, capers, and red onion. Garnish with the fresh dill and serve.

Popcorn Chicken Bites

Prep Time: 10 minutes | Cook Time: 8 minutes | Serves: 2-4

1 pound chicken breasts, cutlets or tenders
1 cup buttermilk
3 to 6 dashes hot sauce (optional)
8 cups cornflakes (or 2 cups cornflake crumbs)
½ teaspoon salt
1 tablespoon butter, melted
2 tablespoons chopped fresh parsley

1. Cut the chicken into bite-sized pieces (about 1-inch) and place them in a bowl with the buttermilk and hot sauce (if using). Cover and let the chicken marinate in the buttermilk for 1 to 3 hours in the refrigerator.
2. Crush the cornflakes into fine crumbs by either crushing them with your hands in a bowl, rolling them with a rolling pin in a plastic bag or processing them in a food processor. Place the crumbs in a bowl, add the melted butter, salt, and parsley and mix well.
3. Working in batches, remove the chicken from the buttermilk marinade, letting any excess drip off and transfer the chicken to the cornflakes. Toss the chicken pieces in the cornflake mixture to coat evenly, pressing the crumbs onto the chicken.
4. Place the chicken in the air fryer basket.
5. Select AIR FRY, set temperature to 380°F, and set time to 8 minutes. Press START/STOP to begin preheating.
6. When the unit has preheated, place the basket into the upper rails of the oven. Toss the chicken halfway through the cooking process.
7. Serve the popcorn chicken bites warm with BBQ sauce or honey mustard for dipping.

Classic Pepperoni Pizza

Prep Time: 15 minutes | Cook Time: 12-15 minutes | Serves: 4

1 pound pizza dough (store-bought or homemade)
½ cup pizza sauce
1½ cups shredded mozzarella cheese
20 slices pepperoni
1 tablespoon olive oil
½ teaspoon dried oregano
¼ teaspoon crushed red pepper flakes (optional)

1. Lightly coat the sheet pan with olive oil and set aside.
2. Roll out the pizza dough on a floured surface to fit the size of the sheet pan. Transfer the dough to the prepared pan.
3. Spread the pizza sauce evenly over the dough, leaving a 1-inch border around the edges.
4. Sprinkle the shredded mozzarella cheese evenly over the sauce, then arrange the pepperoni slices on top.
5. Drizzle a little olive oil over the pizza and sprinkle with the dried oregano and red pepper flakes if desired.
6. Select Pizza, set temperature to 400°F, and set time to 12 minutes. Press START/STOP to begin preheating.
7. When the unit has preheated, place the sheet pan on wire rack into the bottom rails. Bake for 12–15 minutes or until the crust is golden and the cheese is melted and bubbly.
8. Remove the pizza from the unit and let it cool for 5 minutes before slicing. Serve warm.

Sausage Stuffed Mushrooms

Prep Time: 10 minutes | Cook Time: 20 minutes | Serves: 6

½ pound ground pork sausage
¼ teaspoon salt
¼ teaspoon garlic powder
2 medium scallions, trimmed and chopped
½ ounce plain pork rinds, finely crushed
1 pound cremini mushrooms, stems removed

1. In a large bowl, mix the sausage, salt, garlic powder, scallions, and pork rinds. Scoop 1 tablespoon mixture into center of each mushroom cap.
2. Place the mushrooms on the sheet pan.
3. Select AIR ROAST, set temperature to 375°F, and set time to 20 minutes. Press START/STOP to begin preheating.
4. When the unit has preheated, place the sheet pan on the wire rack into the bottom rails.
5. Pork will be fully cooked to at least 145°F in the center and browned when done. Serve warm.

Cauliflower Buffalo Bites with Blue Cheese Dipping Sauce

Prep Time: 10 minutes | Cook Time: 25-35 minutes | Serves: 6

For the Buffalo Bites:
1 large head cauliflower, cut into small florets
2 tablespoons olive oil
¾ cup panko bread crumbs, divided
½ cup buffalo wing sauce (such as Frank's RedHot)

For the Blue Cheese Dipping Sauce:
¼ cup crumbled blue cheese
½ cup mayonnaise
½ cup sour cream
Dash hot pepper sauce (such as Tabasco or Crystal; optional)
3 scallions, white and green parts, thinly sliced
Kosher salt
Freshly ground black pepper

To make the buffalo bites:
1. Line the air fryer basket with parchment paper.
2. In a large bowl, add the cauliflower and olive oil and toss to coat. Add ½ cup of bread crumbs and toss to coat.
3. Place the cauliflower in a single layer on the prepared basket. Save the bowl.
4. Select AIR FRY, set temperature to 400°F, and set time to 15 minutes. Press START/STOP to begin preheating.
5. When the unit has preheated, place the basket into the upper rails of the oven. Cook for 15 to 20 minutes, until the florets are somewhat tender.
6. Remove from the basket and place the cauliflower back in the large bowl. Add the buffalo wing sauce and remaining ¼ cup of bread crumbs and toss to coat. Transfer the florets back to the basket and cook for 10 to 15 minutes more, until the edges are crisp.
7. Serve the buffalo bites hot with the dipping sauce alongside.

To make the blue cheese dipping sauce:
1. While the cauliflower roasts, mix well the blue cheese, mayonnaise, sour cream, hot pepper sauce (if using), and scallions in a medium bowl. Taste and season with the salt and pepper.

Bacon-Wrapped Tater Tots

Prep Time: 10 minutes | Cook Time: 13 minutes | Serves: 6

24 frozen tater tots
12 thin-cut slices bacon, cut in half crosswise
½ cup shredded cheddar cheese (about 2 ounces)
¼ cup sliced green onions, for garnish
½ cup full-fat sour cream, for serving

1. Spray the air fryer basket with avocado oil.
2. Wrap a piece of bacon around each tot and secure it with a toothpick. Place the wrapped tots in the basket, leaving space between them.
3. Select AIR FRY, set temperature to 400°F, and set time to 10 minutes. Press START/STOP to begin preheating.
4. When the unit has preheated, place the basket on the top rails while sliding in the sheet pan and wire rack on the bottom rails. Cook for 10 to 13 minutes, until the bacon is crisp to your liking.
5. Transfer the tots to a serving plate and sprinkle the cheese over the hot tots. Garnish with the green onions and serve with the sour cream.

Sweet and Spicy Nuts

Prep Time: 10 minutes | Cook Time: 20 minutes | Serves: 4

1 large egg white
1 tablespoon water
3 cups raw mixed nuts (almonds, cashews, hazelnuts, pecan halves, or walnut halves)
¼ cup granulated sugar
4 ounces ⅓-less-fat cream cheese, at room temperature
2½ ounces (½ cup) lump crabmeat, picked over for bits of shell
2 scallions, chopped
2 garlic cloves, finely minced
2 teaspoons reduced-sodium soy sauce
15 wonton wrappers
1 large egg white, beaten
5 tablespoons Thai sweet chili sauce, for dipping

1. In a medium bowl, combine the cream cheese, crab, scallions, garlic, and soy sauce. Mix with a fork until thoroughly combined.
2. Working with one at a time, place a wonton wrapper on a clean surface, the points facing top and bottom like a diamond. Spoon 1 level tablespoon of the crab mixture onto the center of the wrapper. Dip your finger in a small bowl of water and gently run it along the edges of the wrapper. Take one corner of the wrapper and fold it up to the opposite corner, forming a triangle. Gently press out any air between wrapper and filling and seal the edges. Set aside and repeat with the remaining wrappers and filling. Brush both sides of the wontons with egg white.
3. Working in batches if necessary, arrange a single layer of the wontons in the air fryer basket.
4. Select AIR FRY, set temperature to 340°F, and set time to 8 minutes. Press START/STOP to begin preheating.
5. When the unit has preheated, place the basket into the upper rails of the oven. Cook, until golden brown and crispy, flipping halfway the wontons.
6. Serve the wontons hot with the chili sauce for dipping.

Crispy Ranch Pickles

Prep Time: 10 minutes | Cook Time: 10 minutes | Serves: 4

4 dill pickle spears, halved lengthwise
¼ cup ranch dressing
½ cup all-purpose flour
½ cup grated Parmesan cheese
2 tablespoons dry ranch seasoning

1. Wrap the spears in a kitchen towel for 30 minutes to soak up excess the pickle juice.
2. Pour the ranch dressing into a medium bowl and add pickle spears. In a separate medium bowl, mix the flour, Parmesan, and ranch seasoning.
3. Remove each spear from the ranch dressing and shake off excess. Press gently into the dry mixture to coat all sides. Place the spears in the air fryer basket.
4. Select AIR FRY, set temperature to 400°F, and set time to 10 minutes. Press START/STOP to begin preheating.
5. When the unit has preheated, place the basket into the upper rails of the oven. Turn the spears three times during cooking.
6. When the cooking is complete, serve warm.

Loaded Zucchini Skins

Prep Time: 10 minutes | Cook Time: 13 minutes | Serves: 4

3 slices center-cut bacon
2 large zucchini (about 9 ounces each)
Olive oil spray
¾ teaspoon kosher salt
¼ teaspoon garlic powder
¼ teaspoon sweet paprika
Freshly ground black pepper
1¼ cups (5 ounces) shredded cheddar cheese
8 teaspoons light sour cream or 2% plain Greek yogurt
2 scallions, green tops only, sliced

1. Place the bacon in the air fryer basket.
2. Select AIR FRY, set temperature to 350°F, and set time to 10 minutes. Press START/STOP to begin preheating.
3. When the unit has preheated, place the basket on the top rails while sliding in the sheet pan and wire rack on the bottom rails. Cook, flipping the bacon halfway, until crisp.
4. When done, place the bacon on paper towels to drain, then coarsely chop.
5. Halve the zucchini lengthwise, then crosswise (you'll have 8 pieces). Scoop the pulp out of each piece, leaving a ¼-inch shell on all sides (save the pulp for another use, such as adding to omelets or soup).
6. Place the zucchini skins on a work surface. Spray both sides with olive oil, then season all over with the salt. Season the cut side with the garlic powder, paprika, and pepper to taste. Arrange a single layer of the zucchini on the sheet pan.
7. Select AIR ROAST, set temperature to 350°F, and set time to 8 minutes. Press START/STOP to begin preheating.
8. When the unit has preheated, place the sheet pan on the wire rack into the bottom rails. Cook until crisp-tender.
9. Remove the sheet pan from the unit and place 2½ tablespoons cheddar inside each skin and top with the bacon. Return the stuffed zucchini in a single layer on the sheet pan to the unit. Cook until the cheese is melted, about 2 minutes.
10. Top each with 1 teaspoon sour cream and the scallions and serve immediately.

Crab and Cream Cheese Wontons

Prep Time: 15 minutes | Cook Time: 8 minutes | Serves: 5

½ teaspoon chili powder
¼ teaspoon ground cinnamon
⅛ teaspoon cayenne powder

1. In a medium bowl, whisk the egg white and the water until frothy.
2. Add the nuts to the bowl and toss to coat.
3. In a small bowl, stir the sugar, chili powder, cinnamon, and cayenne until well mixed. Add the sugar mixture to the nuts and toss to coat them thoroughly. Arrange the nuts evenly in a single layer in the air fryer basket.
4. Select AIR FRY, set temperature to 325°F, and set time to 20 minutes. Press START/STOP to begin preheating.
5. When the unit has preheated, place the basket into the upper rails of the oven. Toss after 10 minutes until the nuts are golden brown and dry.
6. Cool the nuts completely in the basket and serve.

Crispy French Fries

Prep Time: 10 minutes | Cook Time: 40 minutes | Serves: 4

1 pound russet potatoes, scrubbed
2 tablespoons olive oil
Sea salt, for seasoning
Oil spray (hand-pumped)

1. Cut the potatoes lengthwise into ¼-inch-wide batons (fries). Place the fries in a large bowl and cover them with cold water and set aside in the refrigerator for 1 hour.
2. Drain the fries and pat them thoroughly with paper towels to get them as dry as possible.
3. Place the fries in a large bowl and add the olive oil. Generously season with salt.
4. Generously spray the air fryer basket with oil and spread the fries in a single layer in the basket. You will have to do this in two batches.
5. Select AIR FRY, set temperature to 375°F, and set time to 10 minutes. Press START/STOP to begin preheating.
6. When the unit has preheated, place the basket into the upper rails of the oven.
7. Toss and cook for an additional 5 minutes until golden and crispy. If the fries are not crispy enough, cook for 5 additional minutes.
8. Repeat with the remaining fries. Serve immediately.

Chapter 4 Poultry Recipes

Paprika Chicken Wings

Prep Time: 10 minutes | Cook Time: 40 minutes | Serves: 2

Oil spray (hand-pumped)
¾ cup all-purpose flour
1 teaspoon garlic powder
1 teaspoon smoked paprika
½ teaspoon sea salt
¼ teaspoon freshly ground black pepper
¼ teaspoon onion powder
2 pounds chicken wing drumettes and flats

1. In a medium bowl, stir the flour, garlic powder, paprika, sea salt, pepper, and onion powder until well mixed.
2. Add half the chicken wings to the bowl and toss to coat with the flour.
3. Spray the air fryer basket with the oil. Working in batches if necessary, arrange the wings in the basket and spray both sides lightly with the oil.
4. Select AIR FRY, set temperature to 400°F, and set time to 20 minutes. Press START/STOP to begin preheating.
5. When the unit has preheated, place the basket on the top rails while sliding in the sheet pan and wire rack on the bottom rails. Cook, turning the wings halfway through, until golden brown and crispy.
6. Repeat with the remaining wings, covering the cooked wings loosely with foil to keep them warm. Serve.

Easy Chicken Fajitas

Prep Time: 10 minutes | Cook Time: 14 minutes | Serves: 4

1 pound chicken breast tenders, chopped into bite-size pieces
½ onion, thinly sliced
½ red bell pepper, seeded and thinly sliced
½ green bell pepper, seeded and thinly sliced
1 tablespoon vegetable oil
1 tablespoon fajita seasoning
1 teaspoon kosher salt
Juice of ½ lime
8 large lettuce leaves
1 cup prepared guacamole

1. In a large bowl, combine the chicken, onion, and peppers. Drizzle with the vegetable oil and toss until thoroughly coated. Add the fajita seasoning and salt and toss again.
2. Place the chicken and vegetables in a single layer on the sheet pan.
3. Select AIR ROAST, set temperature to 400°F, and set time to 14 minutes. Press START/STOP to begin preheating.
4. When the unit has preheated, place the sheet pan on the wire rack into the bottom rails. Cook until a thermometer inserted into the thickest piece of chicken registers 165°F and the vegetables are tender, tossing halfway through the cooking time.
5. Transfer the mixture to a serving platter and drizzle with the fresh lime juice. Serve with the lettuce leaves and top with the guacamole.

Classic Chicken Parmesan

Prep Time: 15 minutes | Cook Time: 20 minutes | Serves: 2

Oil spray (hand-pumped)
½ cup all-purpose flour
2 large eggs
½ cup bread crumbs
⅓ cup grated Parmesan cheese
2 (5-ounce) chicken breasts, halved widthwise
1 cup tomato sauce
¾ cup shredded mozzarella

1. Spread the air fryer basket with the oil.
2. Add the flour to a plate and set it aside.
3. In a small bowl, whisk the eggs until well beaten and place next to the flour.
4. In a medium bowl, stir the bread crumbs and Parmesan and place next to the eggs.
5. Dredge the chicken in the flour, then egg, then the bread crumb mixture.
6. Place the chicken in the basket and spray it on both sides with the oil.
7. Select AIR FRY, set temperature to 400°F, and set time to 15 minutes. Press START/STOP to begin preheating.
8. When the unit has preheated, place the basket into the upper rails of the oven. Cook, turning halfway through, until golden brown.
9. Evenly divide the tomato sauce between the chicken and top with the cheese. Cook for 5 minutes more until the cheese is melted. Serve.

Crispy Chicken Nuggets

Prep Time: 15 minutes | Cook Time: 12 minutes | Serves: 4

1 pound boneless, skinless chicken breast, cut into 1-inch cubes
½ cup all-purpose flour
2 large eggs, beaten
1 cup panko breadcrumbs
½ cup grated Parmesan cheese
1 teaspoon garlic powder
1 teaspoon smoked paprika
½ teaspoon salt
½ teaspoon black pepper
Olive oil spray
Your favorite dipping sauces, for serving

1. Place the flour in a shallow bowl. In another bowl, beat the eggs. In a third bowl, mix together the panko breadcrumbs, Parmesan cheese, garlic powder, paprika, salt, and black pepper.
2. Dredge each chicken cube in the flour, dip into the beaten eggs, and coat with the breadcrumb mixture, pressing gently to adhere.
3. Arrange the coated chicken nuggets in a single layer in the air fryer basket and lightly spray with olive oil.
4. Select AIR FRY, set temperature to 400°F, and set time to 10 minutes. Press START/STOP to begin preheating.
5. When the unit has preheated, place the basket into the upper rails of the oven. Cook for 10-12 minutes, flipping halfway through, until golden brown and crispy, and the internal temperature reaches 165°F.
6. Serve the chicken nuggets hot with your favorite dipping sauces, such as honey mustard, ranch, or barbecue sauce.

Cilantro Lime Chicken Thighs

Prep Time: 10 minutes | Cook Time: 22 minutes | Serves: 4

4 bone-in, skin-on chicken thighs
1 teaspoon baking powder
½ teaspoon garlic powder
2 teaspoons chili powder
1 teaspoon cumin
2 medium limes
¼ cup chopped fresh cilantro

1. Pat the chicken thighs dry and sprinkle with the baking powder.
2. In a small bowl, mix the garlic powder, cumin, chili powder and sprinkle evenly over thighs, gently rubbing on and under chicken skin.
3. Cut one lime in half and squeeze juice over thighs. Place the chicken on the sheet pan.
4. Select AIR ROAST, set temperature to 380°F, and set time to 22 minutes. Press START/STOP to begin preheating.
5. When the unit has preheated, place the sheet pan on the wire rack into the bottom rails.
6. Cut other lime into four wedges for serving and garnish the cooked chicken with wedges and cilantro.

Honey-Glazed Turkey Tenderloins with Carrots and Snap Peas

Prep Time: 10 minutes | Cook Time: 25 minutes | Serves: 4

2 (12-ounce) turkey tenderloins
1 teaspoon kosher salt, divided
3 tablespoons balsamic vinegar
2 tablespoons honey
1 tablespoon Dijon mustard
½ teaspoon dried thyme
6 large carrots, peeled and cut into ¼-inch-thick slices
8 ounces snap peas
1 tablespoon extra-virgin olive oil

1. If your turkey tenderloins are not pre-brined, sprinkle them with ¾ teaspoon of salt. Place the turkey on a sheet pan.
2. In a small bowl, mix the balsamic vinegar, honey, mustard, and thyme.
3. Put the carrots and snap peas in a medium bowl and drizzle with the oil. Add 1 tablespoon of the balsamic mixture and the remaining ¼ teaspoon of salt, and toss to coat. Scatter the vegetables on the sheet pan around the turkey tenderloins. Brush the tenderloins with about half of the remaining balsamic mixture.
4. Select AIR ROAST, set temperature to 375°F, and set time to 10 minutes. Press START/STOP to begin preheating.
5. When the unit has preheated, place the sheet pan on the wire rack into the bottom rails. Roast the turkey and vegetables for 10 to 12 minutes.
6. Remove the sheet pan from the unit. Gently stir the vegetables. Flip the tenderloins and baste them with the remaining balsamic mixture. Cook for another 10 to 15 minutes, until the center of the tenderloins registers 155°F on a meat thermometer.
7. Slice the turkey and serve with the vegetables.

Buffalo Turkey Meatballs

Prep Time: 15 minutes | Cook Time: 15 minutes | Serves: 4

1 pound ground turkey
½ cup panko breadcrumbs
1 large egg
¼ cup crumbled blue cheese
1 teaspoon garlic powder
½ teaspoon onion powder
½ teaspoon salt
¼ teaspoon black pepper
¼ cup buffalo sauce
2 tablespoons melted butter

1. In a bowl, mix turkey, breadcrumbs, egg, blue cheese, onion powder, garlic powder, salt, and pepper.
2. Form the mixture into 1-inch meatballs and place them in the air fryer basket.
3. Select AIR FRY, set temperature to 375°F, and set time to 12 minutes. Press START/STOP to begin preheating.
4. When the unit has preheated, place the basket into the upper rails of the oven. Cook for 12-15 minutes until golden brown and cooked through.
5. Toss the meatballs with the buffalo sauce and melted butter before serving. Serve with the ranch or blue cheese dressing.

Bacon-Wrapped Stuffed Chicken Breasts

Prep Time: 15 minutes | Cook Time: 30 minutes | Serves: 4

½ cup chopped frozen spinach, thawed and squeezed dry
¼ cup cream cheese, softened
¼ cup grated Parmesan cheese
1 jalapeño, seeded and chopped
½ teaspoon kosher salt
1 teaspoon black pepper
2 large boneless, skinless chicken breasts, butterflied and pounded to ½-inch thickness
4 teaspoons salt-free Cajun seasoning
6 slices bacon

1. In a small bowl, combine the spinach, cream cheese, Parmesan cheese, jalapeño, salt, and pepper. Stir until well combined.
2. Place the butterflied chicken breasts on a flat surface. Spread the cream cheese mixture evenly across each piece of chicken. Starting with the narrow end, roll up each chicken breast, ensuring the filling stays inside. Season chicken with the Cajun seasoning, patting it in to ensure it sticks to the meat.
3. Wrap each breast in 3 slices of bacon. Place the chicken breasts on the sheet pan.
4. Select AIR ROAST, set temperature to 350°F, and set time to 30 minutes. Press START/STOP to begin preheating.
5. When the unit has preheated, place the sheet pan on the wire rack into the bottom rails. Use a meat thermometer to ensure the chicken has reached an internal temperature of 165°F.
6. Let the chicken stand for 5 minutes before slicing each rolled-up breast in half to serve.

Parmesan Chicken Fingers

Prep Time: 10 minutes | Cook Time: 10 minutes | Serves: 2-4

½ cup flour
1 teaspoon salt
freshly ground black pepper
2 eggs, beaten
¾ cup seasoned panko breadcrumbs
¾ cup grated Parmesan cheese
8 chicken tenders (about 1 pound) or 2 to 3 boneless, skinless chicken breasts, cut into strips
Vegetable oil
Marinara sauce

1. Set up a dredging station. Combine the flour, salt, and pepper in a shallow dish. Place the beaten eggs in second shallow dish. Mix the panko breadcrumbs and Parmesan cheese in a third shallow dish.
2. Coat the chicken tenders in the flour mixture, then dip into the egg, and finally place dredge in the breadcrumb mixture, pressing the coating onto both sides of the chicken tenders. Arrange the coated chicken tenders on a baking sheet until they are all coated. Spray both sides of the chicken fingers with the vegetable oil.
3. Working in two batches, place the chicken fingers in the air fryer basket.
4. Select AIR FRY, set temperature to 390°F, and set time to 9 minutes. Press START/STOP to begin preheating.
5. When the unit has preheated, place the basket into the upper rails of the oven.
6. Turn the chicken over halfway through the cooking time. Repeat with the remaining chicken.
7. Serve immediately with the marinara sauce, honey-mustard, ketchup or your favorite dipping sauce.

Spiced Chicken Drumsticks

Prep Time: 5 minutes | Cook Time: 20 minutes | Serves: 4

1 teaspoon cumin seeds
1 teaspoon dried oregano
1 teaspoon dried parsley
1 teaspoon ground turmeric
½ teaspoon coriander seeds
1 teaspoon kosher salt
½ teaspoon black peppercorns
½ teaspoon cayenne pepper
¼ cup fresh lime juice
2 tablespoons olive oil
1½ pounds chicken drumsticks

1. In a clean coffee grinder or spice mill, combine the cumin, oregano, parsley, turmeric, coriander seeds, salt, peppercorns, and cayenne. Process until finely ground.
2. In a small bowl, combine the ground spices with the lime juice and oil. Place the chicken in a resealable plastic bag. Add the marinade, seal, and massage until the chicken is well coated. Marinate at room temperature for 30 minutes or in the refrigerator for up to 24 hours.
3. When you are ready to cook, place the drumsticks skin side up on the sheet pan.
4. Select AIR ROAST, set temperature to 400°F, and set time to 20 minutes. Press START/STOP to begin preheating.
5. When the unit has preheated, place the sheet pan on the wire rack into the bottom rails. Cook for 20 to 25 minutes, turning the legs halfway through the cooking time. Use a meat thermometer to ensure that the chicken has reached an internal temperature of 165°F. Serve.

Chicken Cordon Bleu

Prep Time: 20 minutes | Cook Time: 25 minutes | Serves: 4

Oil spray (hand-pumped)
4 (4-ounce) chicken breasts
4 teaspoons Dijon mustard
4 slices Gruyère cheese
4 slices lean ham
1 cup all-purpose flour
2 large eggs
1 cup bread crumbs
½ cup Parmesan cheese

1. Place a chicken breast flat on a clean work surface and cut along the length of the breast, almost in half, holding the knife parallel to the counter. Open the breast up like a book and place it between two pieces of plastic wrap. Pound the chicken breast to about ¼-inch thick with a rolling pin or mallet. Repeat with the remaining breasts.
2. Spread the mustard on each breast, place a piece of cheese and ham in the center, and fold the sides of the breast over the cheese and ham. Roll the breast up from the unfolded sides to form a sealed packet. Secure with a toothpick.
3. Repeat with the remaining breasts.
4. Sprinkle the flour on a plate and set it on your work surface.
5. In a small bowl, whisk the eggs until well beaten and place next to the flour.
6. In a medium bowl, stir the bread crumbs and Parmesan and place next to the eggs.
7. Dredge the chicken rolls in the flour, then egg, then the bread crumb mixture, making sure they are completely breaded.
8. Spray the air fryer basket with the oil. Place the chicken in the basket and spray lightly all over with the oil.
9. Select AIR FRY, set temperature to 350°F, and set time to 25 minutes. Press START/STOP to begin preheating.
10. When the unit has preheated, place the basket into the upper rails of the oven. Turn the chicken halfway through, until golden brown. Serve.

Crispy Chicken Cutlets

Prep Time: 20 minutes | Cook Time: 15 minutes | Serves: 4

2 boneless, skinless chicken breasts, sliced into thin cutlets
1 cup Italian-seasoned breadcrumbs
½ cup grated Parmesan cheese
1 teaspoon dried oregano
1 teaspoon garlic powder
½ teaspoon salt
½ teaspoon black pepper
2 eggs, beaten
¼ cup all-purpose flour
Olive oil spray

1. Dredge each chicken cutlet in flour, dip in beaten eggs, and coat in the breadcrumb mixture.
2. Arrange the cutlets in the air fryer basket and lightly spray with olive oil.
3. Select AIR FRY, set temperature to 400°F, and set time to 12 minutes. Press START/STOP to begin preheating.
4. When the unit has preheated, place the basket into the upper rails of the oven. Cook for 12-15 minutes, flipping halfway, until crispy and golden brown.
5. Serve with the lemon wedges and a side salad.

Honey Mustard Turkey Burgers

Prep Time: 10 minutes | Cook Time: 10 minutes | Serves: 4

1 pound ground turkey
¼ cup breadcrumbs
1 tablespoon honey
1 tablespoon Dijon mustard
½ teaspoon garlic powder
½ teaspoon onion powder
½ teaspoon salt
¼ teaspoon black pepper
4 burger buns
Olive oil spray

1. In a bowl, combine turkey, breadcrumbs, garlic powder, honey, mustard, onion powder, salt, and pepper.
2. Shape into 4 burger patties.
3. Place the patties in the air fryer basket and spray lightly with olive oil.
4. Select AIR FRY, set temperature to 400°F, and set time to 8 minutes. Press START/STOP to begin preheating.
5. When the unit has preheated, place the basket into the upper rails of the oven. Cook for 8-10 minutes, flipping halfway, until golden and cooked through.
6. Serve on the toasted buns with desired toppings like lettuce, tomato, and honey mustard sauce.

Crispy Chicken Meatballs

Prep Time: 15 minutes | Cook Time: 30 minutes | Serves: 4

1 pound lean ground chicken
½ cup bread crumbs
1 large egg
1 scallion, both white and green parts, finely chopped
¼ cup whole milk
¼ cup shredded, unsweetened coconut
1 tablespoon low-sodium soy sauce
1 teaspoon minced garlic
1 teaspoon fresh ginger, peeled and grated
Pinch cayenne powder
Oil spray (hand-pumped)

1. Line the air fryer basket with parchment and set aside.
2. In a large bowl, mix the chicken, bread crumbs, egg, scallion, milk, coconut, soy sauce, garlic, ginger, and cayenne until very well combined.
3. Shape the chicken mixture into 1½-inch balls and place them in a single layer in the basket. Do not overcrowd them.
4. Select AIR FRY, set temperature to 375°F, and set time to 20 minutes. Press START/STOP to begin preheating.
5. When the unit has preheated, place the basket into the upper rails of the oven. Cook for 20 minutes, turning the meatballs halfway through, until they are cooked through and evenly browned. Serve.

Lebanese Turkey Burgers with Tzatziki

Prep Time: 25 minutes | Cook Time: 12 minutes | Serves: 4

For the Tzatziki:
1 large cucumber, peeled and grated (about 2 cups)
2 to 3 cloves garlic, minced
1 cup plain Greek yogurt
1 tablespoon tahini (sesame paste)
1 tablespoon fresh lemon juice
½ teaspoon kosher salt

For the Burgers:
1 pound ground turkey, chicken, or lamb
1 small yellow onion, finely diced
1 clove garlic, minced
2 tablespoons chopped fresh parsley
2 teaspoons Lebanese Seven-Spice Mix
½ teaspoon kosher salt
Vegetable oil spray

For Serving:
4 lettuce leaves or 2 whole-wheat pita breads, halved
8 slices ripe tomato
1 cup baby spinach
⅓ cup crumbled feta cheese

To make the tzatziki:
1. In a medium bowl, stir together all the ingredients until well combined. Cover and chill until ready to serve.

To make the burgers:
1. In a large bowl, combine the ground turkey, onion, garlic, parsley, spice mix, and salt. Mix gently until well combined. Divide the turkey into four portions and form into round patties.
2. Spray the air fryer basket with vegetable oil spray. Place the patties in a single layer in the basket.
3. Select AIR FRY, set temperature to 400°F, and set time to 12 minutes. Press START/STOP to begin preheating.
4. When the unit has preheated, place the basket into the upper rails of the oven. Use a meat thermometer to ensure the burgers have reached an internal temperature of 165°F (for turkey or chicken) or 160°F (for lamb).
5. Place one burger in each lettuce leaf or pita half. Tuck in 2 tomato slices, spinach, cheese, and some tzatziki.

Tandoori Chicken Breasts

Prep Time: 10 minutes | Cook Time: 30 minutes | Serves: 4

1 cup plain Greek yogurt
¼ sweet onion, finely chopped
2 teaspoons garam masala
1 teaspoon minced garlic
1 teaspoon fresh ginger, peeled and grated
½ teaspoon ground cumin
½ teaspoon ground coriander
¼ teaspoon sea salt
⅛ teaspoon cayenne powder
4 (4-ounce) skinless, boneless chicken breasts
Oil spray (hand-pumped)

1. In a medium bowl, whisk the yogurt, onion, garam masala, garlic, ginger, cumin, coriander, salt, and cayenne until well blended. Add the chicken breast, turning to coat.
2. Cover the bowl and refrigerate for at least 3 hours to overnight.
3. Spread the air fryer basket with the oil. Place the chicken breasts in the basket after shaking off the excess marinade. Discard the remaining marinade.
4. Select AIR FRY, set temperature to 400°F, and set time to 25 minutes. Press START/STOP to begin preheating.
5. When the unit has preheated, place the basket on the top rails while sliding in the sheet pan and wire rack on the bottom rails. Cook for 25 to 30 minutes, turning halfway through, until browned with an internal temperature of 165°F. Serve.

Buffalo Chicken Tenders

Prep Time: 15 minutes | Cook Time: 20 minutes | Serves: 4

1 pound boneless, skinless chicken tenders
¼ cup hot sauce
1½ ounces pork rinds, finely ground
1 teaspoon chili powder
1 teaspoon garlic powder

1. Place the chicken tenders in large bowl and pour the hot sauce over them. Toss the tenders in hot sauce, evenly coating.
2. In a separate large bowl, mix the ground pork rinds, chili powder, and garlic powder.
3. Add each tender to the ground pork rinds, covering completely. Wet your hands with water and press down the pork rinds into the chicken.
4. Place the tenders in a single layer in the air fryer basket.
5. Select AIR FRY, set temperature to 375°F, and set time to 20 minutes. Press START/STOP to begin preheating.
6. When the unit has preheated, place the basket into the upper rails of the oven.
7. When done, serve warm.

Pickle Brined Fried Chicken

Prep Time: 10 minutes | Cook Time: 27 minutes | Serves: 4

4 bone-in, skin-on chicken legs, cut into drumsticks and thighs (about 3½ pounds)
pickle juice from a 24-ounce jar of kosher dill pickles
½ cup flour
salt and freshly ground black pepper
2 eggs
1 cup fine breadcrumbs
1 teaspoon salt
1 teaspoon freshly ground black pepper
½ teaspoon ground paprika
⅛ teaspoon ground cayenne pepper
Vegetable or canola oil in a spray bottle

1. Place the chicken in a shallow dish and pour the pickle juice over the top. Cover and transfer the dish to the refrigerator to brine in the pickle juice for 3 to 8 hours.
2. When ready to cook, remove the chicken from the refrigerator to allow it to come to room temperature while you set up a dredging station. Place the flour in a shallow dish and season well with the salt and freshly ground black pepper. Whisk the eggs in a second shallow dish. In a third shallow dish, combine the breadcrumbs, pepper, paprika, salt, and cayenne pepper.
3. Remove the chicken from the pickle brine and gently dry it with a clean kitchen towel. Coat each piece of chicken in the flour, then dip into the egg mixture, and finally press into the breadcrumb mixture to coat the chicken on all sides with breadcrumbs. Arrange the breaded chicken on a sheet pan and spray each piece all over with vegetable oil.
4. Working in two batches, place the chicken thighs and drumsticks in the air fryer basket.
5. Select AIR FRY, set temperature to 370°F, and set time to 10 minutes. Press START/STOP to begin preheating.
6. When the unit has preheated, place the basket into the upper rails of the oven.
7. Gently turn the chicken pieces over and cook for an additional 10 minutes. Remove the chicken pieces and let them rest on the plate – do not cover. Repeat with the remaining chicken, cooking for 20 minutes, turning the chicken pieces over halfway through.
8. Serve warm and enjoy.

Chapter 5 Beef, Pork, and Lamb Recipes

Barbecued Riblets

Prep Time: 10 minutes | Cook Time: 25 minutes | Serves: 4

1 rack pork riblets, cut into individual riblets
1 teaspoon fine sea salt
1 teaspoon ground black pepper
Sauce:
¼ cup apple cider vinegar
¼ cup beef broth
¼ cup powdered sugar
¼ cup tomato sauce
1 teaspoon liquid smoke
1 teaspoon onion powder
2 cloves garlic, minced

1. Spray the sheet pan with avocado oil.
2. Season the riblets well on all sides with the salt and pepper. Place the riblets on the sheet pan.
3. Select AIR ROAST, set temperature to 350°F, and set time to 10 minutes. Press START/STOP to begin preheating.
4. When the unit has preheated, place the sheet pan on the wire rack into the bottom rails. Flip the riblets halfway through.
5. While the riblets cook, mix all the sauce ingredients together in a large bowl.
6. Remove the riblets from the unit and place them in the bowl with the sauce. Stir to coat the riblets in the sauce. Transfer the riblets to the unit and cook for 10 to 15 minutes, until the pork is cooked through and the internal temperature reaches 145°F.
7. Store leftovers in an airtight container in the refrigerator for up to 4 days.

Flavorful Pork Milanese

Prep Time: 10 minutes | Cook Time: 12 minutes | Serves: 4

4 (1-inch) boneless pork chops
Fine sea salt and ground black pepper
2 large eggs
¾ cup powdered Parmesan cheese (about 2¼ ounces) (or pork dust for dairy-free)
Chopped fresh parsley, for garnish
Lemon slices, for serving

1. Spray the air fryer basket with avocado oil.
2. Place the pork chops between 2 sheets of plastic wrap and pound them with the flat side of a meat tenderizer until they're ¼ inch thick. Lightly season both sides of the chops with salt and pepper.
3. Lightly beat the eggs in a shallow bowl. Divide the Parmesan cheese evenly between 2 bowls and set the bowls in this order: Parmesan, eggs, Parmesan. Dredge a chop in the first bowl of Parmesan, then dip it in the eggs, and then dredge it again in the second bowl of Parmesan, making sure both sides and all edges are well coated. Repeat with the remaining chops.
4. Select AIR FRY, set temperature to 400°F, and set time to 12 minutes. Press START/STOP to begin preheating.
5. Place the chops in the basket.
6. When the unit has preheated, place the basket into the upper rails of the oven. Cook until the internal temperature reaches 145°F, flipping the chops halfway through.
7. Garnish with the fresh parsley and serve immediately with the lemon slices. Store leftovers in an airtight container in the refrigerator for up to 3 days.

Italian Stuffed Bell Peppers

Prep Time: 15 minutes | Cook Time: 15 minutes | Serves: 4

1 pound ground pork Italian sausage
½ teaspoon garlic powder
½ teaspoon dried parsley
1 medium Roma tomato, diced
¼ cup chopped onion
4 medium green bell peppers
1 cup shredded mozzarella cheese, divided

1. In a medium skillet over medium heat, brown the ground sausage about 7–10 minutes or until no pink remains. Drain the fat from the skillet.
2. Return the skillet to the stovetop and add garlic powder, parsley, tomato, and onion. Continue cooking for 3–5 minutes.
3. Slice peppers in half and remove the seeds and white membrane.
4. Remove the meat mixture from the stovetop and spoon evenly into pepper halves. Top with the mozzarella. Place the pepper halves in the air fryer basket.
5. Select AIR FRY, set temperature to 350°F, and set time to 15 minutes. Press START/STOP to begin preheating.
6. When the unit has preheated, place the basket into the upper rails of the oven.
7. When done, peppers will be fork tender and cheese will be golden. Serve warm.

Greek Meatballs with Tzatziki Sauce

Prep Time: 10 minutes | Cook Time: 10-15 minutes | Serves: 4

1 pound 85% lean ground beef
1 cup grated zucchini
½ cup crumbled feta cheese
2 tablespoons finely minced red onion
1 teaspoon garlic powder
1 teaspoon dried oregano
1 teaspoon salt
½ teaspoon freshly ground black pepper
2 teaspoons fresh lemon juice
Tzatziki Sauce:
½ cup sour cream
¼ cup grated cucumber
1 tablespoon fresh lemon juice
½ teaspoon garlic powder
½ teaspoon dried dill
½ teaspoon salt
½ teaspoon freshly ground black pepper

1. In a large mixing bowl, combine the beef, zucchini, feta, red onion, garlic powder, oregano, salt, black pepper, and lemon juice. Mix gently until thoroughly combined. Shape the mixture into 1¼-inch meatballs.
2. Working in batches if necessary, place the meatballs in a single layer in the air fryer basket; coat lightly with olive oil spray.
3. Select AIR FRY, set temperature to 350°F, and set time to 10 minutes. Press START/STOP to begin preheating.
4. When the unit has preheated, place the basket into the upper rails of the oven. Cook for 10 to 15 minutes, until the meatballs are browned and a thermometer inserted into the center of a meatball registers 160°F, tuning the meatballs halfway through the cooking time.
To make the tzatziki sauce:
1. In a bowl, combine the sour cream, cucumber, lemon juice, garlic powder, dill, salt, and black pepper. Stir until thoroughly combined.
2. Serve the meatballs with sauce.

Poblano Pepper Cheeseburgers

Prep Time: 10 minutes | Cook Time: 30 minutes | Serves: 4

2 poblano chile peppers
1½ pounds 85% lean ground beef
1 clove garlic, minced
1 teaspoon salt
½ teaspoon freshly ground black pepper
4 slices Cheddar cheese (about 3 ounces)
4 large lettuce leaves

1. Select AIR FRY, set temperature to 400°F, and set time to 20 minutes. Press START/STOP to begin preheating.
2. Place the poblano peppers in the air fryer basket.
3. When the unit has preheated, place the basket into the upper rails of the oven. Cook until peppers are softened and beginning to char, tuning the peppers halfway through the cooking time.
4. Transfer the peppers to a large bowl and cover with a plate. When cool enough to handle, peel off the skin, remove the seeds and stems, and slice into strips. Set aside.
5. Meanwhile, in a large bowl, combine the ground beef, garlic, salt, and pepper. Shape the beef into 4 patties.
6. Lower the temperature to 360°F. Arrange the burgers in a single layer in the basket and cook for 10 minutes, or until a thermometer inserted into the thickest part registers 160°F, tuning the burgers halfway through the cooking time.
7. Top the burgers with the cheese slices and continue cooking for a minute or two, just until the cheese has melted.
8. Serve the burgers on a lettuce leaf topped with the cooked poblano peppers or serve on buns if desired.

Mediterranean-Style Lamb Meatballs

Prep Time: 15 minutes | Cook Time: 12 minutes | Serves: 4

1 pound ground lamb
¼ cup breadcrumbs
2 tablespoons fresh parsley, chopped
1 teaspoon ground cumin
1 teaspoon dried oregano
½ teaspoon garlic powder
½ teaspoon salt
½ teaspoon black pepper
1 large egg, beaten
1 tablespoon olive oil
Tzatziki sauce, for serving

1. In a large bowl, combine the ground lamb, breadcrumbs, parsley, cumin, oregano, garlic powder, salt, pepper, and beaten egg. Mix until well incorporated.
2. Roll the mixture into 1-inch meatballs and place them in the air fryer basket lined with parchment paper.
3. Brush the meatballs lightly with olive oil to ensure crispiness.
4. Select AIR FRY, set temperature to 375°F, and set time to 12 minutes. Press START/STOP to begin preheating.
5. When the unit has preheated, place the basket into the upper rails of the oven. Cook, turning the meatballs halfway through, until golden brown and cooked through (internal temperature of 160°F).
6. Let the meatballs rest for 5 minutes before serving. Serve with the tzatziki sauce and warm pita bread or a side of couscous.

Shawarma Lamb Loin Chops and Potatoes

Prep Time: 10 minutes | Cook Time: 25 minutes | Serves: 4

Nonstick cooking spray
8 (½-inch-thick) lamb loin chops (about 2 pounds)
2 teaspoons kosher salt, divided
⅓ cup plain whole-milk yogurt
2 tablespoons freshly squeezed lemon juice
3 garlic cloves, minced or lightly smashed
1 teaspoon ground cumin
1 teaspoon smoked paprika
¼ teaspoon ground allspice
¼ teaspoon freshly ground black pepper
¼ teaspoon red pepper flakes
12 ounces small red potatoes, quartered
1 tablespoon olive oil

1. Spray the sheet pan with cooking spray.
2. Season the lamb chops on both sides with 1 teaspoon of salt and let sit while you prepare the marinade.
3. In a large bowl, whisk together the yogurt, garlic, cumin, paprika, lemon juice, remaining 1 teaspoon of salt, the allspice, pepper, and red pepper flakes. Pour the marinade into a zip-top bag, leaving 2 tablespoons of marinade in the bowl. Put the lamb chops in the bag. Squeeze out as much air as possible and massage the bag to coat the chops with the marinade. Set aside.
4. Add the potatoes and oil to the bowl with the remaining marinade and toss to coat. Transfer the potatoes to the prepared sheet pan.
5. Select AIR ROAST, set temperature to 375°F, and set time to 15 minutes. Press START/STOP to begin preheating.
6. When the unit has preheated, place the sheet pan on the wire rack into the bottom rails.
7. Remove the sheet pan from the oven. Remove the chops from the marinade, draining off all but a thin coating. Place the chops on the sheet pan with the potatoes (discard the excess marinade).
8. Select Broil, set temperature to HI, and set time to 5 minutes.
9. Place the sheet pan on the wire rack on bottom rails. Press START/STOP to begin cooking. Broil the chops and potatoes for 5 minutes.
10. Flip the chops and stir the potatoes. Broil for another 5 to 6 minutes, until the lamb's internal temperature reads 145°F (for medium-rare). Continue broiling for a few minutes more if you want the meat more done. Let the chops rest for a few minutes, then serve with the potatoes.

Chinese-Style Pork Spareribs

Prep Time: 10 minutes | Cook Time: 30 minutes | Serves: 4

1 tablespoon sesame oil
1 tablespoon fermented black bean paste
1 tablespoon seasoned rice vinegar
1 tablespoon reduced-sodium soy sauce
1 tablespoon powdered sugar
1 teaspoon minced garlic
1 teaspoon grated fresh ginger
2 pounds pork spareribs, cut into small pieces

1. In a small bowl, combine the sesame oil, black bean paste, rice vinegar, soy sauce, sugar, garlic, and ginger. Stir until thoroughly combined. Transfer the marinade to a gallon-size resealable bag and add the ribs. Seal the bag and massage the ribs to coat with the marinade. Refrigerate for at least 4 hours, preferably overnight.
2. Working in batches if necessary, place the ribs in a single layer on the sheet pan.
3. Select Broil, set temperature to LO, and set time to 30 minutes.
4. Place the sheet pan on the wire rack on bottom rails. Press START/STOP to begin cooking. Cook until tender and browned, tuning the ribs halfway through the cooking time. Serve.

Pesto Pork Chops

Prep Time: 5 minutes | Cook Time: 12 minutes | Serves: 2

2 (6-ounce) boneless pork loin chops
2 tablespoons basil pesto

1. Rub the pork chops all over with the pesto and set aside for 15 minutes.
2. Arrange the pork on the sheet pan with no overlap.
3. Select Broil, set temperature to LO, and set time to 12 minutes.
4. Place the sheet pan on the wire rack on bottom rails. Press START/STOP to begin cooking. Cook, turning the chops halfway through, until the chops are lightly browned and have an internal temperature of 145°F.
5. Let the meat rest for 10 minutes and serve.

Roasted Beef and Vegetables

Prep Time: 15 minutes | Cook Time: 20-25 minutes | Serves: 4

For the Beef:
1 pound flank steak or sirloin, thinly sliced against the grain
2 tablespoons olive oil
3 tablespoons soy sauce
1 tablespoon Worcestershire sauce
1 tablespoon balsamic vinegar
2 cloves garlic, minced
1 teaspoon dried oregano
½ teaspoon black pepper
½ teaspoon red pepper flakes (optional)

For the Vegetables:
1 cup baby carrots, halved lengthwise
1 red bell pepper, sliced into strips
1 yellow bell pepper, sliced into strips
1 small red onion, sliced into wedges
1 cup broccoli florets
2 tablespoons olive oil
1 teaspoon garlic powder
1 teaspoon paprika
Salt and pepper to taste

1. In a large bowl, whisk together olive oil, soy sauce, Worcestershire sauce, balsamic vinegar, minced garlic, black pepper, oregano, and red pepper flakes.
2. Add the sliced beef to the marinade, toss to coat, and let sit while you prepare the vegetables (about 10 minutes).
3. In another bowl, combine the carrots, bell peppers, onion, and broccoli.
Drizzle with olive oil, then season with garlic powder, paprika, salt, and pepper. Toss to coat evenly.
4. Lightly coat the sheet pan with nonstick spray. Spread the vegetables evenly across the pan. Arrange the marinated beef slices over the vegetables in a single layer.
5. Select AIR ROAST, set temperature to 400°F, and set time to 10 minutes. Press START/STOP to begin preheating.
6. When the unit has preheated, place the sheet pan on the wire rack into the
bottom rails. Roast for 10 minutes, then remove the pan, toss the vegetables gently, and flip the beef slices.
7. Return the sheet pan to the unit and roast for an additional 10-15 minutes until the beef is cooked to your desired doneness and the vegetables are tender with slight caramelization.
8. Remove from the oven and let rest for a couple of minutes. Garnish with the fresh chopped parsley if desired and serve hot over rice, quinoa, or with crusty bread.

Herbed Lamb Burgers

Prep Time: 15 minutes | Cook Time: 15 minutes | Serves: 4

1 pound lean ground lamb
1 large egg
1 tablespoon fresh parsley, chopped
2 teaspoons fresh mint, chopped
1 teaspoon minced garlic
¼ teaspoon sea salt
⅛ teaspoon freshly ground black pepper
Olive oil spray (hand-pumped)
4 whole-wheat buns
¼ cup store-bought tzatziki sauce
1 tomato, cut into slices
4 thin red onion slices
½ cup shredded lettuce

1. In a large bowl, mix the lamb, egg, parsley, mint, garlic, salt, and pepper. Form the mixture into 4 patties.
2. Place the burger patties in the air fryer basket. Lightly spray the patties with the oil on both sides.
3. Select AIR FRY, set temperature to 400°F, and set time to 15 minutes. Press START/STOP to begin preheating.
4. When the unit has preheated, place the basket into the upper rails of the oven. Turn the burgers halfway through.
5. Serve on the buns topped with the tzatziki sauce, tomato, onion, and lettuce.

Blue Cheese Sirloin Steak Salad

Prep Time: 15 minutes | Cook Time: 22 minutes | Serves: 4

2 tablespoons balsamic vinegar
2 tablespoons red wine vinegar
1 tablespoon Dijon mustard
1 tablespoon powdered sugar
1 teaspoon minced garlic
Sea salt
Freshly ground black pepper
¾ cup extra-virgin olive oil
1 pound boneless sirloin steak
Avocado oil spray
1 small red onion, cut into ¼-inch-thick rounds
6 ounces baby spinach
½ cup cherry tomatoes, halved
3 ounces blue cheese, crumbled

1. In a blender, combine the balsamic vinegar, red wine vinegar, Dijon mustard, sugar, and garlic. Season with the salt and pepper and process until smooth. With the blender running, drizzle in the olive oil. Process until well combined. Transfer to a jar with a tight-fitting lid, and refrigerate until ready to serve (it will keep for up to 2 weeks).
2. Season the steak with the salt and pepper and let sit at room temperature for at least 45 minutes, time permitting.
3. Spray the steak with oil and place it on the sheet pan.
4. Select Broil, set temperature to LO, and set time to 6 minutes.
5. Place the sheet pan on the wire rack on bottom rails. Press START/STOP to begin cooking.
6. Flip the steak and spray it with more oil. Cook for 6 minutes more for medium-rare or until the steak is done to your liking.
7. Transfer the steak to a plate, tent with a piece of aluminum foil, and let it rest.
8. Spray the onion slices with oil and place them in the air fryer basket. Air fry at 400°F for 5 minutes. Flip the onion slices and spray them with more oil. Cook for 5 minutes more.
9. Slice the steak diagonally into thin strips. Place the spinach, cherry tomatoes, onion slices, and steak in a large bowl. Toss with the desired amount of dressing. Sprinkle with the crumbled blue cheese and serve.

Thai Beef Satay with Peanut Sauce

Prep Time: 10 minutes | Cook Time: 2-3 minutes | Serves: 4

Juice of 3 limes
½ cup fresh cilantro
4 cloves garlic
1-inch piece fresh ginger, peeled and chopped
2 tablespoons powdered sugar
2 tablespoons fish sauce
2 tablespoons reduced-sodium soy sauce
1 teaspoon sriracha or chili-garlic sauce
2 teaspoons sesame oil
1½ pounds flank steak, sliced ¼ inch thick against the grain
2 medium cucumbers, peeled and sliced

Peanut Sauce:
½ cup creamy peanut butter
Juice of ½ lime
1 tablespoon reduced-sodium soy sauce
1 teaspoon powdered sugar
1 teaspoon grated fresh ginger
1 teaspoon chili-garlic sauce
⅓ cup water

1. In a food processor or blender, puree the lime juice, cilantro, garlic, ginger, sugar, fish sauce, soy sauce, sriracha, and sesame oil.
2. Place the steak slices into a gallon-size resealable bag and pour the marinade over the top of the meat. Seal the bag and refrigerate for at least an hour or up to 4 hours.
3. To make the peanut sauce: In a medium bowl, combine the peanut butter, lime juice, soy sauce, sugar, ginger, and chili-garlic sauce. Slowly add the water and whisk until smooth. Cover and refrigerate until ready to serve.
4. Discard the marinade and thread the meat slices back and forth onto skewers. Working in batches if necessary, place the satay skewers on the sheet pan.
5. Select Broil, set temperature to HI, and set time to 2 minutes.
6. Place the sheet pan on the wire rack on bottom rails. Press START/STOP to begin cooking. Cook for 2 or 3 minutes until cooked through, turning the skewers halfway through the time.
7. Serve with the peanut sauce and the cucumbers.

Flank Steak with Tomato Corn Salsa

Prep Time: 15 minutes | Cook Time: 20 minutes | Serves: 4

2 large tomatoes, chopped
1 cup fresh (or canned) corn
½ English cucumber, chopped
¼ red onion, chopped
1 tablespoon jalapeño pepper, chopped
1 tablespoon fresh cilantro, chopped
Sea salt, for seasoning
Freshly ground black pepper, for seasoning
1 pound extra-lean beef flank steak, trimmed of fat
Olive oil, for brushing
1 teaspoon garlic powder
1 teaspoon chili powder

1. In a small bowl, stir the tomato, corn, cucumber, onion, jalapeño, and cilantro, and season with salt and pepper.
2. Rub the steak all over with the oil and then season with the garlic powder, chili powder, salt, and pepper. Transfer the steak to the sheet pan.
3. Select Broil, set temperature to LO, and set time to 20 minutes.
4. Place the sheet pan on the wire rack on bottom rails. Press START/STOP to begin cooking. Cook, turning the steak halfway through, until browned and with an internal temperature of 140°F, for medium-rare.
5. Let the steak rest for 10 minutes and then cut it very thinly against the grain.
6. Serve with the salsa.

Chicken-Fried Steak with Gravy

Prep Time: 15 minutes | Cook Time: 16 minutes | Serves: 2

For the Steak:
Oil spray (hand-pumped)
1 cup all-purpose flour
1 teaspoon garlic powder
1 teaspoon onion powder
1 teaspoon smoked paprika
2 large eggs
2 (½-pound) cube steaks
Sea salt, for seasoning
Freshly ground black pepper, for seasoning

For the Gravy:
2 tablespoons salted butter
2 tablespoons all-purpose flour
1½ cups whole milk
¼ cup heavy (whipping) cream
Sea salt, for seasoning
Freshly ground black pepper, for seasoning

To make the steak:
1. In a medium bowl, stir the flour, garlic powder, paprika, and onion powder until well blended.
2. In a medium bowl, beat the eggs and place them next to the flour.
3. Season the steaks all over with the salt and pepper.
4. Dredge a steak in the egg and then in the flour mixture, making sure it is well coated. Shake off any excess flour.
5. Place the steak in the air fryer basket sprayed with the oil and repeat the process with the other steak. Spray the tops of the steaks with the oil. Cook in batches if necessary.
6. Select AIR FRY, set temperature to 400°F, and set time to 9 minutes. Press START/STOP to begin preheating.
7. When the unit has preheated, place the basket into the upper rails of the oven. Cook until golden brown and crispy.
8. Turn the steaks over, spray the second side with the oil, and cook for an additional 7 minutes.
9. Set the steaks aside to rest for 5 minutes.

To make the gravy:
1. While the steak is cooking, melt the butter in a medium saucepan over medium-high heat.
2. Whisk in the flour and cook for 2 minutes until lightly browned.
3. Whisk in the milk until the gravy is creamy and thick, about 5 minutes. Whisk in the cream and season with the salt and pepper.
4. Serve the steak topped with the gravy.

Parmesan Pork Chops

Prep Time: 15 minutes | Cook Time: 9-14 minutes | Serves: 4

2 large eggs
½ cup finely grated Parmesan cheese
½ cup all-purpose flour
1 teaspoon paprika
½ teaspoon dried oregano
½ teaspoon garlic powder
Salt
Freshly ground black pepper
1¼ pounds (1-inch-thick) boneless pork chops
Avocado oil spray

1. Beat the eggs in a shallow bowl. In a separate bowl, mix the Parmesan cheese, all-purpose flour, paprika, oregano, garlic powder, and salt and pepper to taste.
2. Dip the pork chops into the eggs, then coat them with the Parmesan mixture, gently pressing the coating onto the meat. Spray the breaded pork chops with oil.
3. Place the pork chops in the air fryer basket in a single layer, working in batches if necessary.
4. Select AIR FRY, set temperature to 400°F, and set time to 6 minutes. Press START/STOP to begin preheating.
5. When the unit has preheated, place the basket into the upper rails of the oven.
6. Flip the chops and spray them with more oil. Cook for another 3 to 8 minutes, until an instant-read thermometer reads 145°F.
7. Allow the pork chops to rest for at least 5 minutes, then serve.

Chapter 6 Fish and Seafood Recipes

Crispy Coconut Shrimp

Prep Time: 15 minutes | Cook Time: 17 minutes | Serves: 4

¾ cup unsweetened shredded coconut
¾ cup coconut flour
1 teaspoon garlic powder
¼ teaspoon cayenne pepper
Sea salt
Freshly ground black pepper
2 large eggs
1 pound fresh extra-large or jumbo shrimp, peeled and deveined
Avocado oil spray

1. In a medium bowl, combine the shredded coconut, coconut flour, garlic powder, and cayenne pepper. Season to taste with the salt and pepper.
2. In a small bowl, beat the eggs.
3. Pat the shrimp dry with paper towels. Dip each shrimp in the eggs and then the coconut mixture. Gently press the coating to the shrimp to help it adhere.
4. Select AIR FRY, set temperature to 400°F, and set time to 9 minutes. Press START/STOP to begin preheating.
5. Spray the shrimp with oil and place them in a single layer in the air fryer basket, working in batches if necessary.
6. When the unit has preheated, place the basket into the upper rails of the oven.
7. Then flip and spray them with more oil. Cook for 8 minutes more, until the center of the shrimp is opaque and cooked through.

Halibut Tacos

Prep Time: 20 minutes | Cook Time: 15 minutes | Serves: 4

Oil spray (hand-pumped)
1 teaspoon ground cumin
¼ teaspoon sea salt
⅛ teaspoon freshly ground black pepper
4 (4-ounce) halibut fillets
1 tablespoon olive oil
1 cup red cabbage, shredded
1 carrot, shredded
1 scallion, white and green parts, finely chopped
¼ cup sour cream
Juice of 1 lime
⅛ teaspoon chili powder
4 (8-inch) corn tortillas, room temperature

1. Spray the air fryer basket generously with the oil.
2. In a small bowl, stir the cumin, salt, and pepper until well blended.
3. Season the fish all over with the seasoning mixture.
4. Select AIR FRY, set temperature to 350°F, and set time to 15 minutes. Press START/STOP to begin preheating.
5. Place the fish in the basket and drizzle with the olive oil.
6. When the unit has preheated, place the basket into the upper rails of the oven. Cook for 15 minutes until cooked through and lightly browned.
7. While the fish is cooking, in a medium bowl, toss together the cabbage, sour cream, carrot, scallion, lime juice, and chili powder until very well mixed. Set aside.
8. When done, divide the fish among the tortillas and top with the slaw. Serve.

Maple-Balsamic Glazed Salmon

Prep Time: 10 minutes | Cook Time: 10 minutes | Serves: 4

4 (6-ounce) fillets of salmon
Salt and freshly ground black pepper
Vegetable oil
¼ cup pure maple syrup
3 tablespoons balsamic vinegar
1 teaspoon Dijon mustard

1. Season the salmon well with the salt and freshly ground black pepper. Spray or brush the bottom of the sheet pan with vegetable oil and place the salmon fillets inside.
2. Select Broil, set temperature to HI, and set time to 10 minutes.
3. Place the sheet pan on the wire rack on bottom rails. Press START/STOP to begin cooking.
4. While the salmon is cooking, combine the maple syrup, balsamic vinegar, and Dijon mustard in a small saucepan over medium heat and stir to blend well. Let the mixture simmer while the fish is cooking. It should start to thicken slightly, but keep your eye on it so it doesn't burn.
5. Brush the glaze on the salmon fillets and cook for another 5 minutes. The salmon should feel firm to the touch when finished and the glaze should be nicely browned on top. Brush a little more glaze on top before removing and serving with rice and vegetables, or a nice green salad.

Broiled Tuna Steaks with Roasted Asparagus

Prep Time: 10 minutes | Cook Time: 20 minutes | Serves: 4

1 pound asparagus, trimmed
8 tablespoons olive oil, divided
1 teaspoon kosher salt, divided
1 garlic clove, minced
2 tablespoons freshly squeezed lemon juice
¼ cup chopped fresh parsley, divided
2 tablespoons drained capers
½ teaspoon freshly ground black pepper
4 (8-ounce) tuna steaks, about ¾-inch thick

1. Arrange the asparagus on the sheet pan and drizzle with 1 tablespoon of oil. Toss to coat and sprinkle with ½ teaspoon of salt.
2. Select AIR ROAST, set temperature to 400°F, and set time to 7 minutes. Press START/STOP to begin preheating.
3. When the unit has preheated, place the sheet pan on the wire rack into the bottom rails. Roast the asparagus for 7 to 10 minutes depending on thickness, until just barely tender.
4. Meanwhile, in a small saucepan, heat 3 tablespoons of the remaining oil over low heat. Add the garlic and sauté just until fragrant. Stir in the lemon juice, half the parsley, and capers. Remove the pan from the heat and set aside.
5. Remove the sheet pan from the unit. Rub the remaining 4 tablespoons of oil over both sides of the tuna steaks, and sprinkle with the remaining ½ teaspoon of salt and the pepper. Place the tuna steaks in a single layer on top of the asparagus.
6. Select Broil, set temperature to HI, and set time to 8 minutes. Place the sheet pan on the wire rack on bottom rails. Press START/STOP to begin cooking. Broil for 8 to 10 minutes, turning the fish carefully about halfway through the cooking time. The tuna steaks should still be pink in the middle, and the asparagus should be tender and browned in spots.
7. To serve, drizzle the warm lemon-caper sauce over the tuna and asparagus, then sprinkle the remaining parsley over the fish.

Roasted Cod with Mixed Vegetables

Prep Time: 15 minutes | Cook Time: 20 minutes | Serves: 4

1 small eggplant, peeled and cut into ½-inch-thick slices
1 small zucchini, cut into ½-inch-thick slices
2 teaspoons kosher salt, divided
1 small onion, chopped (about 1 cup)
3 garlic cloves, minced
1 small green bell pepper, seeded and cut into ½-inch chunks (about 1 cup)
1 small red bell pepper, cut into ½-inch chunks (about 1 cup)
½ teaspoon dried oregano
¼ teaspoon freshly ground black pepper
2 tablespoons extra-virgin olive oil
1 pint cherry tomatoes, halved
4 (6-ounce) cod fillets, or other white fish such as tilapia, haddock, and snapper
⅓ cup pesto, plus more for serving (optional)

1. Salt one side of the eggplant and zucchini slices with ¾ teaspoon of salt. Place the slices salted-side down on paper towels. Salt the other sides with another ¾ teaspoon of salt. Let the slices sit for 10 minutes, or until they start to exude water. Rinse and blot dry with more paper towels. Cut the zucchini slices into quarters and the eggplant slices into eighths.
2. Transfer the zucchini and eggplant to the sheet pan and add the onion, garlic, and bell peppers. Drizzle with the oil and sprinkle with the oregano and black pepper, tossing to coat.
3. Select AIR ROAST, set temperature to 375°F, and set time to 8 minutes. Press START/STOP to begin preheating.
4. When the unit has preheated, place the sheet pan on the wire rack into the bottom rails.
5. After roasting for 8 minutes, stir the tomatoes into the vegetable mixture. Place the cod fillets in a single layer on top of the vegetables and sprinkle with the remaining ½ teaspoon of salt. Drizzle the pesto over the fish and vegetables, using a basting brush to spread the pesto evenly over the fillets.
6. Roast for 12 minutes, or until the fish flakes easily with a fork.
7. To serve, spoon the vegetables onto a platter and top with the fish fillets, with additional pesto on the side, if desired.

Garlic Lemon Scallops

Prep Time: 5 minutes | Cook Time: 10 minutes | Serves: 4

4 tablespoons salted butter, melted
4 teaspoons peeled and finely minced garlic
½ small lemon, zested and juiced
8 (1-ounce) sea scallops, cleaned and patted dry
¼ teaspoon salt
¼ teaspoon ground black pepper

1. In a small bowl, mix the butter, garlic, lemon zest, and lemon juice. Place the scallops on the sheet pan. Pour the butter mixture over scallops, then sprinkle with the salt and pepper.
2. Select Broil, set temperature to HI, and set time to 10 minutes.
3. Place the sheet pan on the wire rack on bottom rails. Press START/STOP to begin cooking.
4. Scallops will be opaque and firm, and have an internal temperature of 130°F when done. Serve warm.

Crispy Parmesan Tilapia

Prep Time: 10 minutes | Cook Time: 12 minutes | Serves: 2

2 tilapia fillets (about 6 ounces each)
½ cup grated Parmesan cheese
¼ cup whole-wheat breadcrumbs
1 teaspoon garlic powder
½ teaspoon smoked paprika
½ teaspoon salt
¼ teaspoon black pepper
1 large egg, beaten
Olive oil spray
Lemon wedges, for serving

1. In a shallow dish, combine the Parmesan cheese, breadcrumbs, garlic powder, paprika, salt, and black pepper.
2. Dip each tilapia fillet into the beaten egg, then coat evenly with the Parmesan mixture, pressing lightly to adhere.
3. Select AIR FRY, set temperature to 400°F, and set time to 10 minutes. Press START/STOP to begin preheating.
4. Lightly spray the air fryer basket with olive oil and place the fillets inside.
5. When the unit has preheated, place the basket into the upper rails of the oven. Cook for 10–12 minutes, flipping halfway through, until the fillets are golden brown and crispy.
6. Remove from the unit and serve with the lemon wedges for a fresh touch.

Chilean Sea Bass with Olive Relish

Prep Time: 10 minutes | Cook Time: 10 minutes | Serves: 2

Olive oil spray
2 (6-ounce) Chilean sea bass fillets or other firm-fleshed white fish
3 tablespoons extra-virgin olive oil
½ teaspoon ground cumin
½ teaspoon kosher salt
½ teaspoon black pepper
⅓ cup pitted green olives, diced
¼ cup finely diced onion
1 teaspoon chopped capers

1. Spray the sheet pan with the olive oil spray. Drizzle the fillets with the olive oil and sprinkle with the cumin, salt, and pepper. Place the fish on the sheet pan.
2. Select Broil, set temperature to LO, and set time to 10 minutes.
3. Place the sheet pan on the wire rack on bottom rails. Press START/STOP to begin cooking. Cook until the fish flakes easily with a fork.
4. Meanwhile, in a small bowl, stir together the olives, onion, and capers.
5. Serve the fish topped with the relish.

Homemade Catfish Strips

Prep Time: 15 minutes | Cook Time: 18-20 minutes | Serves: 4

1 cup buttermilk
5 catfish fillets, cut into 1½-inch strips
Olive oil
1 cup cornmeal
1 tablespoon Creole, Cajun, or Old Bay seasoning

1. Pour the buttermilk into a shallow baking dish. Place the catfish in the dish and refrigerate for at least 1 hour to help remove any fishy taste.
2. Spray the air fryer basket lightly with olive oil.
3. In a shallow bowl, combine cornmeal and Creole seasoning.
4. Shake any excess buttermilk off the catfish. Place each strip in the cornmeal mixture and coat completely. Press the cornmeal into the catfish gently to help it stick.
5. Place the strips in the basket in a single layer. Lightly spray the catfish with olive oil. You may need to cook the catfish in more than one batch.
6. Select AIR FRY, set temperature to 400°F, and set time to 8 minutes. Press START/STOP to begin preheating.
7. When the unit has preheated, place the basket into the upper rails of the oven.
8. Turn the catfish strips over and lightly spray with olive oil. Cook until golden brown and crispy, 8 to 10 more minutes.

Fish Fillets with Lemon-Dill Sauce

Prep Time: 5 minutes | Cook Time: 7 minutes | Serves: 4

1 pound snapper, grouper, or salmon fillets
Sea salt
Freshly ground black pepper
1 tablespoon avocado oil
¼ cup sour cream
¼ cup sugar-free mayonnaise (homemade or store-bought)
2 tablespoons fresh dill, chopped, plus more for garnish
1 tablespoon freshly squeezed lemon juice
½ teaspoon grated lemon zest

1. Pat the fish dry with paper towels and season well with the salt and pepper. Brush with the avocado oil.
2. Select Broil, set temperature to HI, and set time to 1 minute.
3. Place the fillets on the sheet pan. Place the sheet pan on the wire rack on bottom rails. Press START/STOP to begin cooking.
4. Set temperature to LO and continue cooking for 5 minutes. Flip the fish and cook for 1 minute more or until an instant-read thermometer reads 145°F. (If using salmon, cook it to 125°F for medium-rare.)
5. While the fish is cooking, make the sauce by combining the sour cream, mayonnaise, lemon juice, dill, and lemon zest in a medium bowl. Season with the salt and pepper and stir until combined. Refrigerate until ready to serve.
6. Serve the fish with the sauce, garnished with the remaining dill.

Crispy Fish and Chips

Prep Time: 25 minutes | Cook Time: 35 minutes | Serves: 4

For the Chips:
1 tablespoon olive oil, plus more for spraying
2 large russet potatoes, scrubbed
1 teaspoon salt
½ teaspoon freshly ground black pepper

For the Fish:
Olive oil
4 (4-ounce) cod fillets
1½ teaspoons salt, divided plus more as needed
1½ teaspoons black pepper, divided, plus more as needed
½ cup whole-wheat flour
2 eggs
1½ cups whole-wheat panko bread crumbs
¼ teaspoon cayenne pepper

To make the chips:
1. Spray the air fryer basket lightly with olive oil.
2. Cut the potatoes lengthwise into ½-inch-thick slices and then into ½-inch-thick fries.
3. In a large bowl, mix together the oil, salt, and pepper and toss with the potatoes to coat.
4. Place the potatoes in a single layer in the basket. You may need to cook them in batches.
5. Select AIR FRY, set temperature to 400°F, and set time to 5 minutes. Press START/STOP to begin preheating.
6. When the unit has preheated, place the basket into the upper rails of the oven.
7. Flip and cook until the potatoes are lightly browned and crisp, 5 to 10 more minutes. Set aside and keep warm.

To make the fish:
1. Spray the air fryer basket with olive oil.
2. Season the fillets with salt and black pepper.
3. In a shallow bowl, mix together the whole-wheat flour, ½ teaspoon of salt, and ½ teaspoon of black pepper.
4. In a second bowl, whisk together the eggs, 1 teaspoon of water, and a pinch of salt and pepper.
5. In another shallow bowl, combine the panko bread crumbs, cayenne pepper, and remaining 1 teaspoon of salt and 1 teaspoon of black pepper.
6. Coat each fillet in the seasoned flour, then coat with the egg, and finally dredge in the panko bread crumb mixture.
7. Place the fillets in the basket in a single layer. Lightly spray the fish with olive oil. You may need to cook them in batches.
8. Cook at 400°F for 8 to 10 minutes. Turn the fillets over and lightly spray with olive oil. Cook until golden brown and crispy, 5 to 10 more minutes.

Crispy Tuna Patties

Prep Time: 15 minutes | Cook Time: 15 minutes | Serves: 4

3 (5-ounce) cans tuna, packed in water
⅔ cup whole-wheat panko bread crumbs
⅓ cup shredded Parmesan cheese
1 tablespoon sriracha
¾ teaspoon black pepper
10 whole-wheat slider buns

1. Spray the air fryer basket lightly with olive oil.
2. In a medium bowl combine the tuna, bread crumbs, Parmesan cheese, sriracha, and black pepper and stir to combine.
3. Form the mixture into 10 patties.
4. Place the patties in the basket in a single layer. Spray the patties lightly with olive oil. You may need to cook them in batches.
5. Select AIR FRY, set temperature to 350°F, and set time to 6 minutes. Press START/STOP to begin preheating. Cook for 6 to 8 minutes.
6. Turn the patties over and lightly spray with olive oil. Cook until golden brown and crisp, another 4 to 7 more minutes.

Crab Cakes

Prep Time: 10 minutes | Cook Time: 10 minutes | Serves: 2-4

1 teaspoon butter
⅓ cup finely diced onion
⅓ cup finely diced celery
¼ cup mayonnaise
1 teaspoon Dijon mustard
1 egg
Pinch ground cayenne pepper
1 teaspoon salt
Freshly ground black pepper
16 ounces lump crabmeat
½ cup + 2 tablespoons panko breadcrumbs, divided

1. In a skillet over medium heat, melt the butter. Sauté the onion and celery until it starts to soften, but not brown, about 4 minutes. Transfer the cooked vegetables to a large bowl. Add the mayonnaise, Dijon mustard, egg, cayenne pepper, salt and freshly ground black pepper to the bowl. Gently add the lump crabmeat and 2 tablespoons of panko breadcrumbs. Stir carefully so you don't break up all the crab pieces.
2. Place the remaining panko breadcrumbs in a shallow dish. Divide the crab mixture into 4 portions and shape each portion into a round patty. Dredge the crab patties in the breadcrumbs, coating both sides as well as the edges with the crumbs. Place the patties in the air fryer basket.
3. Select AIR FRY, set temperature to 400°F, and set time to 8 minutes. Press START/STOP to begin preheating.
4. When the unit has preheated, place the basket into the upper rails of the oven.
5. Using a flat spatula, gently turn the cakes over and cook for another 5 minutes.
6. Serve the crab cakes with tartar sauce or cocktail sauce.

Savory Tandoori Shrimp

Prep Time: 10 minutes | Cook Time: 6 minutes | Serves: 4

1 pound jumbo raw shrimp (21 to 25 count), peeled and deveined
1 tablespoon minced fresh ginger
3 cloves garlic, minced
¼ cup chopped fresh cilantro or parsley, plus more for garnish
1 teaspoon ground turmeric
1 teaspoon Garam Masala
1 teaspoon smoked paprika
1 teaspoon kosher salt
½ to 1 teaspoon cayenne pepper
2 tablespoons olive oil (for Paleo) or melted ghee
2 teaspoons fresh lemon juice

1. In a large bowl, combine the shrimp, ginger, garlic, cilantro, turmeric, garam masala, paprika, salt, and cayenne. Toss well to coat. Add the oil or ghee and toss again. Marinate at room temperature for 15 minutes, or cover and refrigerate for up to 8 hours.
2. Place the shrimp in a single layer in the air fryer basket.
3. Select AIR FRY, set temperature to 325°F, and set time to 6 minutes. Press START/STOP to begin preheating.
4. When the unit has preheated, place the basket into the upper rails of the oven.
5. Transfer the shrimp to a serving platter. Cover and let the shrimp finish cooking in the residual heat, about 5 minutes.
6. Sprinkle the shrimp with the lemon juice and toss to coat. Garnish with additional cilantro and serve.

Smoked Salmon Phyllo Triangles

Prep Time: 15 minutes | Cook Time: 10 minutes | Serves: 6

4 ounces smoked salmon, flaked or chopped
4 ounces cream cheese, softened
2 scallions, chopped
12 sheets phyllo dough, thawed
½ cup (1 stick) unsalted butter, melted

1. Line the air fryer basket with parchment paper.
2. In a small bowl, mash the salmon, cream cheese, and scallions into a rough paste.
3. When you're ready to assemble the triangles, have the melted butter ready, and open the package of dough. Phyllo dries out easily, so don't open it until you're ready to use it. While assembling the triangles, cover the rest of the dough with plastic wrap to keep it from drying out.
4. Unfold the phyllo and cut each sheet lengthwise into two long strips (it's easiest to do this in two or three batches). Lay out 3 or 4 strips of phyllo on a cutting board with the short end toward you, and brush the strips lightly with melted butter. Using a small spoon, place about 2 teaspoons of the filling in the lower left corner of the phyllo. Spread it out so that it's roughly triangular and covers the corner. Wrap the phyllo up like a flag, using repeated diagonal folds. Place the finished triangle in the prepared basket and brush with a little more butter.
5. Repeat with the remaining phyllo to make 24 triangles.
6. Select AIR FRY, set temperature to 400°F, and set time to 10 minutes. Press START/STOP to begin preheating.
7. When the unit has preheated, place the basket into the upper rails of the oven. Cook for 10 to 12 minutes, until the dough is golden brown and flaky.
8. Let cool for 5 to 7 minutes before serving.

Simple Buttered Cod Fillets

Prep Time: 5 minutes | Cook Time: 8 minutes | Serves: 2

2 (4-ounce) cod fillets
2 tablespoons salted butter, melted
1 teaspoon Old Bay seasoning
½ medium lemon, sliced

1. Place the cod fillets on the sheet pan. Brush each fillet with the butter and sprinkle with the Old Bay seasoning. Lay two lemon slices on each fillet.
2. Select Broil, set temperature to HI, and set time to 8 minutes.
3. Place the sheet pan on the wire rack on bottom rails. Press START/STOP to begin cooking.
4. Flip the cod fillets halfway through the cooking time. When cooked, internal temperature should be at least 145°F. Serve warm.

Chapter 7 Desserts Recipes

Mini Apple Hand Pies

Prep Time: 15 minutes | Cook Time: 12 minutes | Serves: 4

1 refrigerated pie crust, rolled out
1 medium apple, peeled, cored, and diced
2 tablespoons granulated sugar
½ teaspoon ground cinnamon
1 tablespoon all-purpose flour
1 egg, beaten (for egg wash)

1. Roll out the pie crust on a lightly floured surface and cut out circles using a 3 to 4-inch round cookie cutter. Re-roll scraps to cut additional circles as needed.
2. In a bowl, combine the diced apple, sugar, cinnamon, and flour. Mix well to evenly coat the apples.
3. Place about 1 tablespoon of apple filling in the center of each dough circle. Fold the dough over the filling to create a half-moon shape and press the edges with a fork to seal tightly.
4. Brush the tops of the pies with beaten egg for a golden finish.
5. Lightly grease the air fryer basket or line it with parchment paper. Place the hand pies in a single layer, ensuring space between them for even cooking.
6. Select AIR FRY, set temperature to 375°F, and set time to 12 minutes. Press START/STOP to begin preheating.
7. When the unit has preheated, place the basket into the upper rails of the oven. Cook until the crust is golden brown and crisp.
8. Let the pies cool for a few minutes before serving. Serve warm, optionally dusted with the powdered sugar or paired with vanilla ice cream.

Brownie Bites

Prep Time: 10 minutes | Cook Time: 15 minutes | Serves: 6

½ cup unsalted butter, melted
¾ cup granulated sugar
2 large eggs
1 teaspoon vanilla extract
⅓ cup unsweetened cocoa powder
½ cup all-purpose flour
¼ teaspoon salt
Cooking spray for greasing

1. In a bowl, stir together the melted butter and sugar until well combined.
2. Add the eggs one at a time, whisking well after each addition. Stir in the vanilla extract.
3. In a separate bowl, sift together the cocoa powder, flour, and salt.
4. Gradually fold the dry ingredients into the wet ingredients, stirring until just combined.
5. Grease the muffin cups, then spoon the brownie batter into each cup, filling them about ¾ full. Place the muffin cups on the sheet pan.
6. Select BAKE, set temperature to 350°F, and set time to 15 minutes. Press START/STOP to begin preheating.
7. When the unit has preheated, place the sheet pan on wire rack into the bottom rails. Bake until a toothpick inserted in the center comes out with a few moist crumbs.
8. Allow the brownie bites to cool for 5 minutes before serving.

Soft Pretzels

Prep Time: 20 minutes | Cook Time: 15 minutes | Serves: 4

½ cup warm water plus 2 quarts water, for boiling
2 tablespoons sugar
1½ teaspoons kosher salt, plus more for sprinkling
1 (¼-ounce) packet active dry yeast
4 cups all-purpose flour
Nonstick cooking spray
½ cup baking soda
1 large egg, beaten

1. In a large bowl, combine ½ cup of warm water, sugar, and kosher salt. Stir in the yeast and let the mixture rest until it starts to foam. Stir in the flour, then transfer the dough to a floured board and knead for 6 to 8 minutes, until the dough is smooth. Wipe out the bowl and spray with cooking spray. Return the dough to the bowl and cover with plastic wrap or a clean towel. Let rest in a warm place for 35 to 40 minutes, until the dough has risen by about half.
2. Line the sheet pan with parchment paper.
3. In a large pot, bring the 2 quarts of water and baking soda to a boil.
4. Meanwhile, punch the dough down and divide it into 8 pieces. Roll out each piece into a 24-inch rope. One at a time, shape the pretzels. Bring the ends toward yourself into an upside-down horseshoe. Cross one side over the other, then cross the second side back over the first to form a traditional pretzel twist. Press the ends against the dough to seal. Place on the prepared sheet pan and repeat with the remaining ropes.
5. Gently lower the pretzels into the boiling water, one or two at a time, and boil for 20 to 30 seconds. Using a large slotted spatula, remove them from the water and place them back on the sheet pan.
6. Brush the tops of the pretzels with the beaten egg and sprinkle with additional kosher salt. Working in batches, place the pretzels on the sheet pan.
7. Select BAKE, set temperature to 400°F, and set time to 12 minutes. Press START/STOP to begin preheating.
8. When the unit has preheated, place the sheet pan on wire rack into the bottom rails. Bake for 12 to 14 minutes, until dark golden brown.
9. Let cool for a minute, then transfer to a rack for 5 to 10 minutes.

Cream Cheese Cookies

Prep Time: 15 minutes | Cook Time: 12-15 minutes | Serves: 12

½ cup unsalted butter, softened
4 ounces plain cream cheese, softened
1 cup granulated sugar
2 eggs
1 tablespoon vanilla extract
1 teaspoon salt
6 cups all-purpose flour

1. Line the sheet pan with parchment paper.
2. In a stand mixer fitted with a paddle attachment, beat the butter, sugar, and cream cheese until fluffy. Beat in the eggs, vanilla extract, and salt. Set the mixer to the lowest speed and slowly add the all-purpose flour, ½ cup at a time, until thoroughly combined. (The dough will be dense and crumbly.)
3. Working in batches if necessary, roll a spoonful of dough into a ball, flatten it between your palms, and arrange on the sheet pan (leave enough space between the cookies so they don't touch).
4. Select BAKE, set temperature to 350°F, and set time to 12 minutes. Press START/STOP to begin preheating.
5. When the unit has preheated, place the sheet pan on wire rack into the bottom rails. Bake for 12 to 15 minutes until the edges are lightly golden.
6. Cool completely before removing from the unit (the cookies will harden as they cool).

Carrot Cake with Cream Cheese Icing

Prep Time: 5 minutes | Cook Time: 55 minutes | Serves: 6-8

1¼ cups all-purpose flour
1 teaspoon baking powder
½ teaspoon baking soda
1 teaspoon ground cinnamon
¼ teaspoon ground nutmeg
¼ teaspoon salt
2 cups grated carrot (about 3 to 4 medium carrots or 2 large)
¾ cup granulated sugar
¼ cup brown sugar
2 eggs
¾ cup canola or vegetable oil
For the Icing:
8 ounces cream cheese, softened at room temperature
8 tablespoons butter (4 ounces or 1 stick), softened at room temperature
1 cup powdered sugar
1 teaspoon pure vanilla extract

1. Grease a cake pan that fits your unit.
2. Combine the flour, baking powder, baking soda, cinnamon, nutmeg and salt in a bowl. Add the grated carrots and toss well. In a separate bowl, beat the sugars and eggs together until light and frothy. Drizzle in the oil, beating constantly. Fold the egg mixture into the dry ingredients until everything is just combined and you no longer see any traces of flour. Pour the batter into the cake pan and wrap the pan completely in greased aluminum foil.
3. Select BAKE, set temperature to 400°F, and set time to 40 minutes. Press START/STOP to begin preheating.
4. When the unit has preheated, place the cake pan on wire rack into the bottom rails.
5. After 40 minutes, remove the aluminum foil cover and bake for an additional 15 minutes or until a skewer inserted into the center of the cake comes out clean and the top is nicely browned.
6. While the cake is baking, beat the cream cheese, butter, powdered sugar, and vanilla extract together using a hand mixer, stand mixer or food processor (or a lot of elbow grease!).
7. Remove the cake pan from the unit and let the cake cool in the cake pan for 10 minutes or so. Then remove the cake from the pan and let it continue to cool completely. Frost the cake with the cream cheese icing and serve.

Buttermilk Biscuits

Prep Time: 15 minutes | Cook Time: 15 minutes | Serves: 4

3 cups all-purpose flour, plus more for the work surface
1½ tablespoons sugar
1½ teaspoons kosher salt
1 tablespoon baking powder
¾ teaspoon baking soda
12 tablespoons (1½ sticks) cold, unsalted butter, cut into ½-inch pieces, plus
2 tablespoons melted unsalted butter, for brushing
1 cup plus 2 tablespoons buttermilk

1. In a medium bowl, whisk the flour, sugar, salt, baking powder, and baking soda to combine well.
2. Using a pastry cutter, two knives, or a mixing blade attachment on your mixer, cut the cold butter into the dry ingredients until the mixture forms coarse crumbs.
3. Add the buttermilk and, using your hands, quickly mix the buttermilk into the dry ingredients until the mixture comes together in a sticky dough.
4. On a floured surface, press or pat the dough until it is about ½ inch thick, and fold it over itself. Pat out the dough and fold it over two or three more times. Finally, pat out the dough into an even ¾-inch thickness. Using a 3-inch round biscuit cutter or cookie cutter, cut out 12 biscuits. Arrange them on the sheet pan. Brush the melted butter over the tops.
5. Select BAKE, set temperature to 375°F, and set time to 13 minutes. Press START/STOP to begin preheating.
6. When the unit has preheated, place the sheet pan on wire rack into the bottom rails. Bake for 13 to 15 minutes, until the biscuits are puffed and golden brown on the outside.
7. Serve immediately.

Nutella & Strawberry Toast

Prep Time: 5 minutes | Cook Time: 3 minutes | Serves: 2

4 slices brioche bread
½ cup Nutella
6 strawberries, sliced
1 tablespoon powdered sugar

1. Select Toast, set the number of bread slices to 4, and set the shade level to your preference.
2. Place the bread slices on the wire rack into bottom rails. Press the START/STOP button to begin cooking. Toast for 3 minutes.
3. Spread the Nutella on warm toast and top with the strawberry slices. Sprinkle with the powdered sugar and serve.

Lemon Blueberry Scones

Prep Time: 15 minutes | Cook Time: 12 minutes | Serves: 6

2 cups all-purpose flour
¼ cup granulated sugar
1 tablespoon baking powder
¼ teaspoon salt
½ cup unsalted butter, cold and cubed
1 cup fresh blueberries
Zest of 1 lemon
½ cup heavy cream (plus extra for brushing)
1 large egg
1 teaspoon vanilla extract

1. In a large bowl, whisk together the flour, sugar, baking powder, and salt.
2. Add the cold butter cubes and use your fingers or a pastry cutter to mix until the mixture resembles coarse crumbs.
3. Gently fold in the blueberries and lemon zest, ensuring the berries remain intact.
4. In a separate bowl, stir together the heavy cream, egg, and vanilla extract. Gradually pour the wet mixture into the dry ingredients and stir until a dough forms.
5. Transfer the dough onto a floured surface, gently knead it a few times, and shape it into a 1-inch thick round disk. Cut into 6 equal wedges.
6. Line the sheet pan with parchment paper and arrange the scones evenly apart. Brush the tops with extra heavy cream for a golden finish.
7. Select BAKE, set temperature to 375°F, and set time to 12 minutes. Press START/STOP to begin preheating.
8. When the unit has preheated, place the sheet pan on wire rack into the bottom rails. Bake until golden brown.
9. Let the scones cool for 5 minutes before serving with butter or glaze if desired.

Mini Chocolate Nut Pies

Prep Time: 15 minutes | Cook Time: 25 minutes | Serves: 10

1¼ cups pecans
½ teaspoon sea salt
1 egg white
1¼ cups macadamia nuts, pecans, or a combination
⅓ cup plus 2 tablespoons sweetened chocolate chips
½ cup brown sugar
3 tablespoons maple syrup
2 tablespoons unsalted butter
2 tablespoons heavy (whipping) cream
1 teaspoon vanilla extract
2 large eggs, beaten

1. Place the pecans and salt in the bowl of a food processor. Process until the nuts are very finely chopped. Transfer to a small bowl.
2. Place the egg white in the bowl of an electric mixer, and mix at high speed until stiff peaks form. Stir the egg white into the chopped pecans. Press the mixture into the bottom of 10 silicone muffin cups. Place the muffin cups in the air fryer basket in a single layer, working in batches if necessary.
3. Select AIR FRY, set temperature to 300°F, and set time to 7 minutes. Press START/STOP to begin preheating.
4. When the unit has preheated, place the basket into the upper rails of the oven.
5. Remove the air fryer basket from the unit. Allow the muffin cups to cool slightly before removing them from the basket.
6. While the crusts are cooling, pulse the macadamia nuts in the food processor until coarsely chopped. Transfer to a medium bowl and toss with 2 tablespoons of chocolate chips. Divide the mixture among the muffin cups.
7. Place the brown sugar, maple syrup, and butter in a small saucepan over medium-high heat. Cook until the butter is melted and the sugars are dissolved. Stir in the cream and vanilla. Remove the pan from the heat and allow the mixture to cool slightly, then stir in the beaten eggs.
8. Pour the mixture over the nuts in the muffin cups, and return the basket with muffin cups to the unit. Set the temperature to 300°F and cook for 12 minutes. Once the pies are cool enough to handle, remove them from the basket.
9. Place the remaining ⅓ cup of chocolate chips in a glass bowl, and heat them in the microwave for about 1 minute, until melted. Stir well. (You can also melt the chocolate in the top of a double boiler.) Drizzle the chocolate over the pies and allow it to set before serving.

Hasselback Apple Crisp

Prep Time: 5 minutes | Cook Time: 20 minutes | Serves: 4

2 large Gala apples, peeled, cored and cut in half
¼ cup butter, melted
½ teaspoon ground cinnamon
2 tablespoons sugar
Topping:
3 tablespoons butter, melted
2 tablespoons brown sugar
¼ cup chopped pecans
2 tablespoons rolled oats
1 tablespoon flour
Vanilla ice cream
Caramel sauce

1. Place the apples cut side down on a cutting board. Slicing from stem end to blossom end, make 8 to 10 slits down the apple halves but only slice three quarters of the way through the apple, not all the way through to the cutting board.
2. Transfer the apples to the sheet pan, flat side down. Combine ¼ cup of melted butter, cinnamon and sugar in a small bowl. Brush this butter mixture onto the apples.
3. Select BAKE, set temperature to 330°F, and set time to 15 minutes. Press START/STOP to begin preheating.
4. When the unit has preheated, place the sheet pan on wire rack into the bottom rails. Baste the apples several times with the butter mixture during the cooking process.
5. While the apples are baking, make the filling. Combine 3 tablespoons of melted butter with the brown sugar, pecans, rolled oats, and flour in a bowl. Stir with a fork until the mixture resembles small crumbles.
6. Spoon the topping down the center of the apples and continue to cook for an additional 5 minutes.
7. Transfer the apples to a serving plate and serve with the vanilla ice cream and caramel sauce.

Air Fried Beignets

Prep Time: 5 minutes | Cook Time: 5 minutes | Serves: 4-6

¾ cup lukewarm water (about 90°F)
¼ cup sugar
1 generous teaspoon active dry yeast (½ envelope)
3½ to 4 cups all-purpose flour
½ teaspoon salt
2 tablespoons unsalted butter, room temperature and cut into small pieces
1 egg, lightly beaten
½ cup evaporated milk
¼ cup melted butter
1 cup confectioners' sugar
Chocolate sauce or raspberry sauce, to dip

1. Mix the lukewarm water, a pinch of the sugar and the yeast in a bowl and allow it to proof for 5 minutes. It should froth a little. If it doesn't froth, your yeast is not active and you should start again with new yeast.
2. Combine 3½ cups of the flour, salt, 2 tablespoons of butter and the remaining sugar in a large bowl, or in the bowl of a stand mixer. Add the egg, evaporated milk and yeast mixture to the bowl and mix with a wooden spoon (or the paddle attachment of the stand mixer) until the dough comes together in a sticky ball. Add a little more flour if necessary to get the dough to form. Transfer the dough to an oiled bowl, cover with plastic wrap or a clean kitchen towel and let it rise in a warm place for at least 2 hours or until it has doubled in size. The longer it takes, the better it is for flavor development. You can even let the dough rest in the refrigerator overnight (just remember to bring it to room temperature before continuing).
3. Roll the dough out to ½-inch thickness. Cut the dough into rectangular or diamond-shaped pieces. You can make the beignets any size you like, but this recipe makes 24 (2-inch x 3-inch) rectangles.
4. Brush the beignets on both sides with some of the melted butter and place them on the air fryer basket, working in batches if necessary.
5. Select AIR FRY, set temperature to 350°F, and set time to 5 minutes. Press START/STOP to begin preheating.
6. When the unit has preheated, place the basket into the upper rails of the oven. Turn the beignets over halfway through if desired. They will brown on all sides without being flipped, but flipping them will brown them more evenly.
7. Once the beignets are finished, transfer to a plate or baking sheet and dust with the confectioners' sugar. Serve warm with a chocolate or raspberry sauce.

Peanut Butter Banana Toast

Prep Time: 5 minutes | Cook Time: 3 minutes | Serves: 2

2 slices whole wheat bread
2 tablespoons peanut butter
1 banana, sliced
1 teaspoon honey
A pinch of cinnamon

1. Select Toast, set the number of bread slices to 2, and set the shade level to your preference.
2. Place the bread slices on the wire rack into bottom rails. Press the START/STOP button to begin cooking. Toast for 3 minutes.
3. Spread the peanut butter evenly on each slice. Layer the banana slices on top and drizzle with the honey. Sprinkle with the cinnamon and serve warm.

Ham and Cheese Croissants

Prep Time: 10 minutes | Cook Time: 8 minutes | Serves: 4

4 store-bought croissants
4 slices ham
4 slices Swiss cheese
1 tablespoon Dijon mustard (optional)

1. Slice the croissants in half and spread the Dijon mustard on one side (if using).
2. Add a slice of ham and cheese to each.
3. Select Toast, set the number of bread slices to 6, and set the shade level to your preference.
4. Working in batches, place the bread slices on the wire rack into bottom rails. Press the START/STOP button to begin cooking. Toast for 8 minutes.
5. When done, serve warm.

Authentic Struffoli

Prep Time: 15 minutes | Cook Time: 20 minutes | Serves: 4-6

¼ cup butter, softened
⅔ cup sugar
5 eggs
2 teaspoons vanilla extract
Zest of 1 lemon
4 cups all-purpose flour
2 teaspoons baking soda
¼ teaspoon salt
16 ounces honey
1 teaspoon ground cinnamon
Zest of 1 orange
2 tablespoons water
Nonpareils candy sprinkles

1. Cream the butter and sugar together in a bowl until light and fluffy using a hand mixer (or a stand mixer). Add the eggs, lemon zest, and vanilla and mix. In a separate bowl, combine the flour, salt, and baking soda. Add the dry ingredients to the wet ingredients and mix until you have a soft dough. Shape the dough into a ball, wrap it in plastic and let it rest for 30 minutes.
2. Divide the dough ball into four pieces. Roll each piece into a long rope. Cut each rope into about 25 (½-inch) pieces. Roll each piece into a tight ball. You should have 100 little balls when finished.
3. In batches if necessary, transfer the dough balls to the air fryer basket, leaving a small space in between them.
4. Select AIR FRY, set temperature to 375°F, and set time to 3 minutes. Press START/STOP to begin preheating.
5. When the unit has preheated, place the basket into the upper rails of the oven. Cook the dough balls for 3 to 4 minutes, flipping when one minute of cooking time remains.
6. After all the dough balls are cooked, make the honey topping. Melt the honey in a small saucepan on the stovetop. Add the cinnamon, orange zest, and water. Simmer for one minute. Place the air-fried dough balls in a large bowl and drizzle the honey mixture over top. Gently toss to coat all the dough balls evenly. Transfer the coated struffoli to a platter and sprinkle the nonpareil candy sprinkles over top. You can dress the presentation up by piling the balls into the shape of a wreath or pile them high in a cone shape to resemble a Christmas tree.
7. Struffoli can be made ahead. Store covered tightly.

Nutmeg Butter Cookies

Prep Time: 10 minutes | Cook Time: 10 minutes | Serves: 8

½ cup (1 stick) unsalted butter, melted
1 cup sugar
1 teaspoon vanilla extract
¼ teaspoon kosher salt
1 large egg
1 cup all-purpose flour
1½ teaspoons freshly grated nutmeg

1. Line the sheet pan with parchment paper.
2. In a large bowl, mix together the butter and sugar. Stir in the vanilla and salt. Add the egg and beat until the mixture is smooth.
3. In a small bowl, whisk together the flour and nutmeg. Stir the flour mixture into the sugar and butter mixture just until blended.
4. Drop the batter by level teaspoons onto the prepared sheet pan, leaving about 2 inches around the dough balls.
5. Select BAKE, set temperature to 350°F, and set time to 11 minutes. Press START/STOP to begin preheating.
6. When the unit has preheated, place the sheet pan on wire rack into the bottom rails. Bake for 11 to 12 minutes, or until the cookies have spread, the edges are golden brown, and the tops start to collapse.
7. Let cool on the sheet pan for a few minutes, then transfer to a rack to cool completely.

Crispy Coconut Bananas with Pineapple Sauce

Prep Time: 5 minutes | Cook Time: 5 minutes | Serves: 4

3 firm bananas
¼ cup sweetened condensed milk
1¼ cups shredded coconut
⅓ cup crushed graham crackers (crumbs)
Vegetable or canola oil, in a spray bottle
Vanilla frozen yogurt or ice cream
Pineapple Sauce:
1½ cups puréed fresh pineapple
2 tablespoons sugar
Juice of 1 lemon
¼ teaspoon ground cinnamon

1. Make the pineapple sauce by combining the pineapple, sugar, lemon juice and cinnamon in a saucepan. Simmer the mixture on the stovetop for 20 minutes, and then set it aside.
2. Slice the bananas diagonally into ½-inch thick slices and place them in a bowl. Pour the sweetened condensed milk into the bowl and toss the bananas gently to coat. Combine the coconut and graham cracker crumbs together in a shallow dish. Remove the banana slices from the condensed milk and let any excess milk drip off. Dip the banana slices in the coconut and crumb mixture to coat both sides. Spray the coated slices with oil.
3. Select AIR FRY, set temperature to 400°F, and set time to 5 minutes. Press START/STOP to begin preheating.
4. Grease the air fry basket with a little oil and place the banana in the basket.
5. When the unit has preheated, place the basket into the upper rails of the oven. Cook until the bananas are golden brown on both sides, turning them over halfway through the cooking time.
6. Serve warm over vanilla frozen yogurt with some of the pineapple sauce spooned over top.

Conclusion

Congratulations on exploring the incredible versatility of your Ninja Flip Toaster Oven & Air Fryer with this colorful cookbook! By now, you've discovered how easy it is to create restaurant-quality meals right in your own kitchen. From crispy appetizers to wholesome dinners and indulgent desserts, the possibilities are endless—and delicious.

But this is just the beginning. As you continue to experiment, don't be afraid to get creative. Adjust the flavors, try new ingredients, and personalize the recipes to suit your taste. The Ninja Flip Toaster Oven & Air Fryer isn't just a kitchen appliance; it's your tool for culinary exploration, helping you achieve crispy, golden perfection with less oil and more flavor.

We hope this cookbook has inspired you to enjoy healthier, faster, and more satisfying meals. Keep it handy whenever you need a quick breakfast, a cozy dinner, or a fun snack. Share your creations with friends and family, and watch as your Ninja Flip Toaster Oven & Air Fryer becomes the star of your kitchen.

Thank you for choosing this cookbook. Here's to many more delicious meals, healthier cooking habits, and joyful kitchen adventures ahead!

Appendix 1 Measurement Conversion Chart

VOLUME EQUIVALENTS (LIQUID)

US STANDARD	US STANDARD (OUNCES)	METRIC (APPROXIMATE)
2 tablespoons	1 fl.oz	30 mL
¼ cup	2 fl.oz	60 mL
½ cup	4 fl.oz	120 mL
1 cup	8 fl.oz	240 mL
1½ cup	12 fl.oz	355 mL
2 cups or 1 pint	16 fl.oz	475 mL
4 cups or 1 quart	32 fl.oz	1 L
1 gallon	128 fl.oz	4 L

TEMPERATURES EQUIVALENTS

FAHRENHEIT (F)	CELSIUS (C) (APPROXIMATE)
225 °F	107 °C
250 °F	120 °C
275 °F	135 °C
300 °F	150 °C
325 °F	160 °C
350 °F	180 °C
375 °F	190 °C
400 °F	205 °C
425 °F	220 °C
450 °F	235 °C
475 °F	245 °C
500 °F	260 °C

VOLUME EQUIVALENTS (DRY)

US STANDARD	METRIC (APPROXIMATE)
⅛ teaspoon	0.5 mL
¼ teaspoon	1 mL
½ teaspoon	2 mL
¾ teaspoon	4 mL
1 teaspoon	5 mL
1 tablespoon	15 mL
¼ cup	59 mL
½ cup	118 mL
¾ cup	177 mL
1 cup	235 mL
2 cups	475 mL
3 cups	700 mL
4 cups	1 L

WEIGHT EQUIVALENTS

US STANDARD	METRIC (APPROXIMATE)
1 ounce	28 g
2 ounces	57 g
5 ounces	142 g
10 ounces	284 g
15 ounces	425 g
16 ounces (1 pound)	455 g
1.5 pounds	680 g
2 pounds	907 g

Appendix 2 Recipes Index

A
Air Fried Beignets 63
Authentic Struffoli 64
Avocado and Egg Breakfast Bagel 9

B
Bacon-Wrapped Jalapeño Poppers 26
Bacon-Wrapped Stuffed Chicken Breasts 36
Bacon-Wrapped Tater Tots 30
Barbecued Riblets 42
Blue Cheese Sirloin Steak Salad 47
Breakfast Calzone 12
Broiled Tuna Steaks with Roasted Asparagus 51
Brownie Bites 58
Buffalo Chicken Tenders 41
Buffalo Turkey Meatballs 36
Buttermilk Biscuits 60

C
Carrot Cake with Cream Cheese Icing 60
Carrots with Cumin-Orange Vinaigrette 21
Cauliflower Buffalo Bites with Blue Cheese Dipping Sauce 29
Cauliflower Steak with Gremolata 18
Cheesy Bell Pepper Eggs 14
Cheesy Broccoli Sticks 24
Cheesy Olive and Roasted Pepper Bread 10
Cherry Tomato Avocado Toast 16
Chicken Cordon Bleu 38
Chicken-Fried Steak with Gravy 49
Chilean Sea Bass with Olive Relish 53
Chinese-Style Pork Spareribs 45
Cilantro Lime Chicken Thighs 35
Cinnamon Rolls with Cream Cheese Glaze 16
Classic Chicken Parmesan 34
Classic Pepperoni Pizza 28
Crab and Cream Cheese Wontons 32
Crab Cakes 56
Cranberry Orange Muffins 12
Cream Cheese Cookies 59
Crispy Breakfast Quesadilla 10
Crispy Chicken Cutlets 38
Crispy Chicken Meatballs 39
Crispy Chicken Nuggets 34
Crispy Coconut Bananas with Pineapple Sauce 65
Crispy Coconut Shrimp 50
Crispy Fish and Chips 55
Crispy French Fries 32
Crispy Nacho Avocado Fries 27
Crispy Parmesan Artichokes 25
Crispy Parmesan Tilapia 53
Crispy Ranch Pickles 31
Crispy Tuna Patties 55

D
Dry Rub Chicken Wings 25

E
Easy Chicken Fajitas 33
Egg-Loaded Potato Skins 11

F
Fish Fillets with Lemon-Dill Sauce 54
Flank Steak with Tomato Corn Salsa 48
Flavorful Pork Milanese 42
French Toast Casserole 15

G
Garlic Lemon Scallops 52
Greek Meatballs with Tzatziki Sauce 43

H
Halibut Tacos 50
Ham and Cheese Croissants 64
Ham and Cheese Pastries 13
Ham and Egg Cups 13
Hasselback Apple Crisp 62
Healthy Bell Pepper Salad 19
Herbed Lamb Burgers 47
Herbed Shiitake Mushrooms 20
Homemade Catfish Strips 54
Honey Mustard Turkey Burgers 39
Honey-Glazed Turkey Tenderloins with Carrots and Snap Peas 35

I
Italian Stuffed Bell Peppers 43

J
Jalapeño Popper Egg Cups 11

L
Lebanese Turkey Burgers with Tzatziki 40
Lemon Blueberry Scones 61
Lemon Thyme Asparagus 18
Lemony Blueberry Muffins 9
Loaded Zucchini Skins 31

M
Maple-Balsamic Glazed Salmon 51
Mediterranean-Style Lamb Meatballs 44
Mini Apple Hand Pies 58
Mini Chocolate Nut Pies 62
Mini Hasselback Potatoes 17
Mozzarella Sticks 26

N
Nutella & Strawberry Toast 61
Nutmeg Butter Cookies 65

P
Paprika Chicken Wings 33
Parmesan Chicken Fingers 37
Parmesan Pork Chops 49
Parsnip Fries with Romesco Sauce 24
Peanut Butter Banana Toast 63
Pesto Pork Chops 46
Pickle Brined Fried Chicken 41
Poblano Pepper Cheeseburgers 44
Popcorn Chicken Bites 28

R
Ratatouille Vegetables 19
Roasted Beef and Vegetables 46
Roasted Cod with Mixed Vegetables 52
Roasted Rosemary Potatoes 21

S
Sausage Cheddar Scones 14
Sausage Cheese Balls 15
Sausage Stuffed Mushrooms 29
Savory Tandoori Shrimp 56
Sesame Green Beans 23
Shawarma Lamb Loin Chops and Potatoes 45
Shishito Peppers with Sour Cream Dipping Sauce 20
Simple Buttered Cod Fillets 57
Smoked Salmon & Cream Cheese Bagel 27
Smoked Salmon Phyllo Triangles 57
Soft Pretzels 59
Spiced Chicken Drumsticks 37
Spicy Vegetable and Tofu 23
Sweet and Sour Brussels Sprouts 22
Sweet and Spicy Nuts 30

T
Tandoori Chicken Breasts 40
Thai Beef Satay with Peanut Sauce 48

V
Veggie Burgers 22

Z
Zucchini Salad with Feta and Parsley 17